STOCK INVESTING STRATEGIES

How to approach stock
investing without getting lost in the
details ...

Maria Crawford Scott

Editor, *AAII Journal*

John Bajkowski

Editor, *Computerized Investing*
Senior Financial Analyst

"The American Association of Individual Investors is an independent, not-for-profit corporation formed in 1978 for the purpose of assisting individuals in becoming effective managers of their own assets through programs of education, information, and research."

For more information about membership, contact:

American Association of Individual Investors
625 N. Michigan Avenue
Chicago, Ill. 60611
(312) 280-0170
(800) 428-2244
www.aaii.com
ISBN: 1-883328-10-1

CONTENTS

The Basic Process Used in Fundamental Analysis

One of the biggest difficulties for individuals interested in investing in stocks is getting started. Many books have been written about each and every aspect of fundamental stock analysis. These books walk investors through the fine details of corporate financial statements, comparative financial ratios, all kinds of stock screens and every imaginable valuation model. The detail and complexity often leaves newcomers perplexed, wondering: Where do I begin, what is important, and how do I apply it to my situation?

In this book, we will provide a general outline for analyzing stocks and walk through the process as it is practically applied to specific types of investment approaches. To achieve this without getting bogged down in details, we will use a somewhat simplistic approach; from that base, you can build up your knowledge of the details, because in the real world marketplace, you will be competing with those who know all of the details. In the end, you should have a general understanding of fundamental stock analysis and its practical application.

We will first describe, in very broad terms, the basic process that is followed in fundamental analysis. Then we will go into the various steps in more detail and show how they can be adapted and practically applied to an individual's specific approach using commonly-found information sources. Most chapters will have an accompanying appendix that more fully explains the screen and the problems you might run into when applying it to a large database using a computer. Appendix A describes the uses of a computer in fundamental analysis and screening, and lists the popular software programs designed for these purposes.

THE BASIC PROCESS

When buying a stock, an investor faces the same question that the purchaser of any good faces: Is this good worth the price being asked? Judging the worth or value of a stock is the basic aim of stock analysis. And to reach this aim using a fundamental approach, stock analysis follows this basic process:

- Since it isn't practical to judge the worth of every single stock in existence, you must start with a limited list of stocks that are promising investment candidates. How do you come up with this list? You might simply start with one or several stocks that someone has recommended or that for one reason or another piqued

Fundamental Stock Analysis: The Basic Process

Initial investment criteria and stock screening: Developing a list of promising candidates using criteria based on return needs, risk tolerance and investment philosophy. Defines your overall investment approach.

Financial statement and ratio analysis: Gathering information on and analyzing the financial condition of a company and its ability to produce earnings to help form reasonable expectations concerning the company's financial future.

Stock valuation: Determining what you feel the stock is worth considering the potential for future price appreciation and dividends.

Final decision: Deciding whether to buy the stock based on your determination of the stock's value relative to the current market price.

your interest. A more methodical approach is to start with a list of stocks that have met certain criteria you set.

- Once you have a manageable-sized list to work with, you must gather information on and analyze the financial condition of the companies on the list.
- The analysis of the firm's financial condition allows you to form expectations concerning its future; based on these expectations, you can put a price on the stock—the amount you feel the stock is worth.
- Your final decision is based on how your estimated valuation compares with the current price of the stock. Your final decision may also be tempered by how confident you are with the information you have received, your analysis, and your expectations.

This short outline, described in layman's terms, is reasonable, logical, and easier said than done.

Let's look at a more formal description of the outline using investment terms for the steps of the process. Not only will this help you better understand the process, it may also help you identify areas you have read about or learned previously but were unclear as to where they fit in the overall stock analysis process.

Initial investment criteria and stock screening: Developing a list of promising candidates. Aside from relying on recommendations, the primary method investors use to develop their initial manageable list of promising stocks is to concentrate on stocks with certain fundamental attributes.

Stock screens are simply criteria that are applied to a broad universe of stocks; the investor can then focus on the narrower list of stocks that pass the criteria. Screening involves scanning through a large universe of stocks, which is done easiest on a computer. Investors who don't use computers can use pre-screened lists that are available or they can develop criteria that stocks must meet before they are considered as candidates.

Obviously, the criteria by which stocks are initially selected are crucial. For the most part, these criteria will be based on your return objectives, tolerance for risk, and investment philosophy. Return objectives encompass not only the total return but also how those returns are achieved—whether solely from price appreciation or a combination of price appreciation and dividend income. Risk tolerance refers to how much volatility of return you can tolerate without panicking. And investment philosophy encompasses the style used to select stocks; it is based in large part on your beliefs as to what drives stock prices. For instance, an investor with a tolerance for greater risk and few income needs may choose criteria that allow him to focus on growth-oriented companies, while an investor with a need for some income and less tolerance for risk may concentrate on stocks with higher dividends and lower price volatility, focusing on utilities with above-average dividend growth rates. This defines your overall investment approach.

Financial statement and ratio analysis: Gathering information on and analyzing the financial condition of a company. Fundamental analysis is premised on the notion that the value or worth of a stock is based in large part on expectations concerning the future performance of the company. Since most investors lack a crystal ball, expectations are derived from a study of the past and current financial condition of the company and its ability to produce earnings.

Corporate financial statements are a key source for evaluating a company's financial condition. However, it's difficult to draw conclusions based solely on the raw numbers—learning that XYZ had net earnings of $19 million in 1995 doesn't add much to an understanding of the firm.

Ratio analysis is the method by which information from the various financial statement accounts can be assessed. Financial ratios are computed from selected information in the annual financial statements; examples that you may be familiar with already include the current ratio (current assets divided by current liabilities, a measure of the firm's ability to meet short-term obligations and operating expenses); return on equity (net profit after taxes divided by stockholders' equity, a measure of profitability); and price-earnings ratio (market price divided by earnings per share, a measure of how the market is currently pricing the stock).

A firm's financial ratios are compared to its historical ratios as well as industry ratios. Comparing financial ratios to historical ratios helps identify important trends, while comparing financial ratios to industry averages allows investors to see how the firm stacks up to competitors. This analysis allows investors to form judgments of the company upon which reasonable expectations can be built.

Stock valuation: Determining what you feel the stock is worth. The goal of stock analysis is to determine a stock value that can be compared to the current market price. Stock valuation is aimed at formulating expectations about the company's future prospects and the potential risk and return behavior of the stock, and converting these expectations into a dollar value through the use of the proper valuation formula.

In practical terms, a stock's risk and return potential is based on expectations of earnings, dividends, cash flow, and asset values. While each of these is interrelated and interdependent, most valuation formulas usually concentrate on one variable. For the individual investor, valuation formulas based on assets or cash flows are impractical because it is difficult to obtain and analyze meaningful data. Information on earnings and dividends, however, is more readily available and presents the most practical base to build upon.

If all companies had similar financial conditions and operated in similar environments, an investor could use one valuation formula in every situation. However, all companies are not similar. They differ in factors such as their stages of development, competitive nature, and industry; certain valuation models are more appropriate for certain firms than they are for others. Stock valuation requires investor judgment at many levels, from determining which valuation models are appropriate for a particular firm, to determining the most reasonable assumptions to use in the formulas such as, should future growth expectations be based on a firm's expected dividend, sales or earnings growth?

The actual decision. Your final decision to invest in a stock will be based on a comparison of the stock's current market price to the value you have placed on the stock. And whether your decision was a good one is obviously dependent on all of the inputs—how promising your initial list was, how accurate the information you compiled on the firm was, how reasonable the assumptions and expectations you developed and used in your valuation formulas were, and whether or not you used appropriate assumptions and formulas in your analysis.

APPLYING THE BASIC APPROACH

How do you apply this process?

As we have seen, determining the initial selection criteria depends heavily on an individual's investment philosophy, risk tolerance and return needs—an individual's overall investment approach. But it's difficult to develop an approach without an understanding of what drives stock prices and valuations.

For that reason, we will take a look at a very basic financial statement, ratio analysis and stock valuation form, to help give you a feel for the driving forces behind stock prices. Then we will look at the various investment approaches, the types of investors who may be drawn to these approaches, and the risk, return and other characteristics of stocks that are initially selected using these approaches. Later chapters will apply that basic form to various investment approaches, discussing which screens or criteria can be applied to draw up an initial list, which financial ratios should be emphasized, which valuation methods are most appropriate, sources of information, and special factors that should be taken into consideration.

This book won't turn you into a financial analyst, but it should give you a foundation upon which to build a practical stock portfolio.

A Simple Worksheet for Evaluating Stocks

Stock selection requires you to gather and analyze data and information in a systematic way. The task of selecting stocks is made easier by organizing the decision process to ensure that salient data and information is evaluated in some logical sequence that allows an investor to make a reasonable decision. The ultimate goal is to determine, through a range of values, what you think the stock is really worth. Let's run through a simplified version of the process, just to get an idea of what occurs.

The accompanying worksheet provides an easy-to-follow format that allows you to walk through the complete process without getting bogged down in complicated financial analysis. However, any final real-world decision would include the further evaluation of other fundamental aspects of the company.

At the bottom of the worksheet, two valuation models are presented, one based on a firm's earnings and the other on its dividends. The two formulas look different, but they are actually quite similar except for the use of earnings in one and dividends in the other. They equate a stock's price to a stream of future earnings or dividends by asking the question: How much are investors paying for this expected stream?

Both models assume that the growth prospects of the firm have not changed fundamentally over time. The historical relationships between the stock's price and earnings or dividends per share can be used to estimate future value. Then, if current market prices differ significantly from the estimated values based on the historical relationships, it means the market, for whatever reason, is evaluating future income potential differently and may be mispricing the security.

The first approach is for stocks with low or non-existent dividends—the traditional growth stock—and is a price-earnings ratio approach. The price-earnings ratio—share price divided by earnings per share—indicates how much investors are willing to pay for each dollar of the firm's earnings. The higher the ratio, the more investors are paying for earnings, with the expectation that those earnings will increase or the more confident they are of earnings predictions. Conversely, lower ratios indicate low earnings expectations or a low confidence in earnings predictability.

For the earnings valuation, the average annual high and low price-earnings ratios are calculated for prior years. Multiplying these historical ranges by an estimate of next year's earnings per share provides an estimate of future value.

Valuation Worksheet

Company _____   Current Price $ _____   Date (_/_/_)

Ticker _____   Exchange _____   Current P/E _____   Current Yield _____

Financial Statement & Ratio Analysis

Per Share Information	Company 19___	19___	19___	19___	19___	5-year avg	Industry or Competitor 19___	5-year avg	Market 19___
Price: High									
Price: Low									
Earnings per Share (EPS)						growth rate:			
Dividends per Share (DPS)						growth rate:			
Book Value per Share (BV)									

Financial Ratios

Price-Earnings Ratio (P/E): Avg*									
High (High Price ÷ EPS)									
Low (Low Price ÷ EPS)									
Dividend Yield % (DY): Avg*									
High (DPS ÷ Low Price)									
Low (DPS ÷ High Price)									
Payout Ratio % (DPS ÷ EPS)									
Return on Equity % (EPS ÷ BV)									
Financial Leverage %									

*Avg = (High + Low) ÷ 2   Shaded areas do not need to be filled in.

Valuation Estimates

Model based on earnings:

Average high P/E × estimated 19___ EPS: _____ × _____ = _____ (high valuation estimate)

Average low P/E × estimated 19___ EPS: _____ × _____ = _____ (low valuation estimate)

Model based on dividends:

Estimated 19___ annual DPS ÷ average low DY**: _____ ÷ _____ = _____ (high valuation estimate)

Estimated 19___ annual DPS ÷ average high DY**: _____ ÷ _____ = _____ (low valuation estimate)

**Use decimal form for DY. For instance 5.4% would be 0.054.

While it may seem difficult to make an earnings estimate, the recent earnings history that is part of the worksheet will give you some basis for forming those expectations. In addition, there are a number of sources where you can obtain analysts' estimates of future earnings, including Value Line and Standard & Poor's. [We will provide a more extensive listing of information sources in the next chapter.]

The second approach is primarily for mature, dividend-paying stocks, such as public utilities, which are generally low-growth stocks. It is a dividend yield approach. Dividend yield—dividends per share divided by share price—is the dividend as a percentage of the stock price. It relates share price to dividends: the *lower* the dividend yield, the greater the emphasis on earnings growth and disregard for dividend income. The *higher* the dividend yield, the lower the expectation of earnings growth and the greater the emphasis on dividend income. At the extreme, a high dividend yield may indicate the expectation of a dividend decrease.

This approach requires an estimate of the next expected annual cash dividend. Again, the recent dividend history in the worksheet should provide you with a feel for changes over time or you can use analysts' estimates.

Dividing the expected annual dividend by the average low dividend yield will give a high-price estimate; dividing the expected annual dividend by the average high dividend yield results in the low-price estimate.

FILLING IN THE NUMBERS

To work through the equations at the bottom of the worksheet, you need to fill out the top section. This section—Financial Statement & Ratio Analysis—collects the information needed in the valuation models and also provides figures that will serve as a financial checklist. This financial checklist helps analyze the assumptions upon which the model is based, since if these assumptions are incorrect, your valuations are invalid.

The figures and ratios you fill in here can be gathered using a company's financial statements, which means you will have to calculate many of the ratios yourself. A better bet, particularly for a beginner, is to use one of the various stock information sources that do much of the legwork for you.

The first section indicates per share information concerning the stock: the high and low share prices for the last five years, as well as earnings per share and dividends per share for each of the last five years. For the earnings per share and dividends per share figure, it is also useful to determine the five-year growth rate. We will discuss how this can be calculated later. This growth rate can then be used to develop your own estimate of next year's earnings and dividends.

The next section lists financial ratios; here, the two primary ratios we are focusing on are the price-earnings ratio and dividend yield. For this model, these two figures should be calculated from the per share data: for price-earnings ratios, divide the high and low share price by the earnings per share; for dividend yield, divide the annual cash dividends by the low and high price. Averages are obtained by adding the yearly figures and dividing by the number of years with valid figures. Note that if earnings are negative or dividends nonexistent, you will be unable to calculate a figure for that year.

Also listed in this form is the payout ratio (dividends per share divided by earnings per share); return on equity (earnings per share divided by book value per share), and financial leverage [such as long-term debt to capitalization (long-term debt plus equity) or long-term debt to equity], which are used as part of your financial checklist. Most of these ratios can be calculated from the per share financial data in this worksheet, or they can be taken from the stock information sources. Financial leverage cannot be calculated by the per share data in this worksheet and the various sources use different measures. For these reasons, it is important to stick to one information source when making comparisons.

Financial ratios for the industry in which the firm operates (or a close competitor) as well as for the market as a whole are listed as part of the checklist.

THE FINANCIAL CHECKLIST

It's easy to compare the valuations you come up with to the current market price. But those valuations are only as good as the inputs and assumptions used in formulating the models.

For instance, the models assume that the firm's growth prospects have not fundamentally changed. But will growth continue at its current pace? The models also assume that historical relationships will continue. But were past relationships affected by a one-time occurrence that is unlikely to continue? Will dividends continue to be paid at the same rate?

Examining the historical patterns of the per share figures and ratios and comparing them to competitors and to industry and market benchmarks are particularly useful in evaluating your inputs and assumptions.

What do you look for and compare? In the simple worksheet presented here, answering the following questions would be appropriate:

- Have earnings grown at a stable rate?
- Have the earnings per share been steady and positive each year, or have they been volatile, making predictions more difficult?
- For dividend-paying firms, has the payout ratio been steady? Increases in the payout ratio, and payout ratios above 100% are an indication that future dividends may go down; high payout ratios mean slower or no dividend growth and perhaps even a decline.
- Is the current price-earnings ratio low relative to the market and industry or a competitor, and does this vary from previous years?
- Is the current dividend yield high relative to the market and industry or a competitor, and does this vary from previous years?
- Has the return on equity, a measure of financial return that provides an indication of how well the firm has used reinvested earnings to generate additional earnings, been high and stable?

- Is the use of financial leverage, a measure of financial risk that indicates how much of the assets of the firm have been financed by debt, low relative to industry norms?

AMERITECH: AN EXAMPLE

An example using Ameritech, with information reported by Value Line, helps illustrate the use of this simple worksheet. The per share information is presented below, along with some selected ratios. All figures have been adjusted, by Value Line, for a 2-for-1 stock split that occurred January 24, 1994.

If you plug these numbers into the worksheet, you will see that the price-earnings ratio model determines a high price of $49.83, a low price of $38.94 and an average price of $44.38, while the dividend model produces a high of $43.91, a low of $34.83 and an average price of $39.37. [You may end up with slightly different numbers due to rounding.] The current price (as of June 30, 1995) is around $44: It's trading within the predicted range of the price-earnings model, but just above the range for the yield-based model.

Ameritech: An Example

	1990	1991	1992	1993	1994
Price: High ($)	34.9	34.9	37.0	45.6	43.1
Price: Low ($)	26.3	27.9	28.1	35.1	36.3
EPS ($)	2.37	2.32	2.51	2.67	3.07
DPS ($)	1.61	1.72	1.78	1.86	1.94
BV ($)	14.63	15.18	12.94	14.35	10.98

Value Line estimated 1995 EPS: $3.30
Value Line estimated 1995 DPS: $2.00

	Ameritech		Industry	
Financial Ratios	1994	5-Yr Avg	1994	4-Yr Avg
Price-Earnings Ratio (x)	13.2	13.4*	13.9	14.8**
Dividend Yield (%)	4.8	5.2*	4.9	4.7**
Payout Ratio (%)	63	69	66	69
Return on Equity (%)	28	19.5	20.4	16.5
Long-Term Debt to Capitalization (%)	42.3	38.7	44.7	44.2

*An average of the 5-year high and 5-year low.
** An average of the last 4 years.

Source: Value Line

Are the assumptions and figures used in the model reasonable? A run through the checklist evaluates this:

- Yearly earnings per share appear to be increasing in a fairly stable pattern (except for 1991), and all of the figures were positive. Value Line's estimate for 1995, however, shows a smaller percentage increase than in the previous year. Further analysis—and understanding Value Line's reasons for this change—would be useful to determine whether or not you agree with Value Line's assessment.
- Ameritech's payout ratio has generally decreased over time and is now below that of the industry. This should enable Ameritech to support its dividend payout or even increase the payout if earnings continue to grow.
- Ameritech's price-earnings ratio is low compared to both its industry and the market (the S&P 500's price-earnings ratio is at 15.4). Its dividend yield is roughly equal to the industry average. Who are those competitors? In the Value Line industry comparisons, many are high-flying cellular stocks, which tend to be higher growth and higher price-earnings ratios.
- Ameritech's return on equity has been stable and increasing and currently exceeds its industry norm. However, Ameritech's long-term debt ratio (Value Line's measure of financial leverage) has increased recently. Fortunately it is slightly lower than the industry average. Companies can boost return on equity by taking on more debt, but they increase their risk to shareholders in the process.

The financial checklist indicates that some of the assumptions in the model are reasonable, but some—such as the Value Line assumptions concerning dividend and earnings growth—should be examined in more detail. A lower 1995 earnings per share estimate would, of course, produce lower valuation estimates.

CONCLUSION

For this particular company, your search may stop here. For stocks that appear more promising, however, you would need to look at other fundamental aspects of the company before any investment decision is made.

For a simple beginning, the worksheet will provide you with an easy-to-follow approach to determining value. The basic format is to:

- Determine which valuation model best suits your needs.
- Determine what information you need to gather for those valuations.
- Determine what information you need to evaluate the assumptions and other inputs used in the models.

Clearly, your information sources play a critical role in the analysis. We will take a closer look at sources of information, and some of the problems and differences you may encounter when using them.

Sources of Information for the Simplified Approach

In the previous chapter, we presented a simplified version of the valuation process, along with a worksheet with two valuation models, one based on a firm's earnings and the other on its dividends. The worksheet provides a systematic approach to gathering information needed for the valuations.

Clearly, the information sources play a critical role in the analysis. Let's take a closer look at sources of information and some of the problems and differences you may encounter when using them.

PER SHARE DATA

Most of the information in a worksheet can be derived from the per share financial information detailed at the top of the worksheet on page 8. This consists of, for each of the last five years: high and low share prices, earnings per share, dividends per share and book value per share.

The primary source for the per share information is the firm's annual financial reports. Corporate annual reports will include both summary and detailed financial statements, although even more detailed financial statements are available in a separate report, the 10K. Both of these reports can be requested from the company.

The detailed financial reports include the standard balance sheets for the last two years listing company assets, liabilities, and shareholder equity; income statements for the last three years listing items such as revenue, expenses, dividend payments, and earnings; statements of shareholders' equity for the last three years, which tracks the flow of funds into and out of shareholders' equity including retained earnings and proceeds from new stock issued or stock option plans; and cash flow statements for the last three years, which examine increases or decreases in cash based on company operations, investing activities, and financial activities.

Also included in the detailed reports—and highly important—are the notes that accompany the statements. The notes will address factors such as whether there were any changes in accounting policies that may impact the statements; a breakdown of inventory; depreciation schedules for property, plant, and equipment; terms of capital leases; detailed tax expense reports; litigations; material business changes such as

Sources for Corporate Financial Information

Moody's Handbook of Common Stock
Financial Information Services
60 Madison Ave., 6th Floor
New York, N.Y. 10010
(212) 413-7700; (800) 342-5647
www.moodys.com
Analyzes over 1,600 common stocks; presents 10 years of data. Also includes some industry information.

Standard & Poor's Stock Reports
65 Broadway, 8th Floor
New York, N.Y. 10006
(800) 221-5277
www.stockinfo.standardpoor.com
Company reports are found in volumes according to the exchange on which they are traded; presents 10 years of data.

Value Line Investment Survey
220 E. 42nd Street
New York, N.Y. 10017-5891
(800) 634-3583; for orders, (800) 833-0046
valueline.com
Analyzes over 1,700 common stocks; presents 15 years of data. Also includes industry information.

acquisitions, investments, and major commitments with other companies; and even a detailed breakdown of long-term debt.

The annual report will also include a summary table that could prove useful in filling out the valuation worksheet. These tables often cover a five- or 10-year span and may include basic data such as earnings per share, dividends per share, and book value per share. Some annual reports will also list historical high and low stock prices. However, there is no consistent format for these tables, and the amount of information provided varies from firm to firm.

Investors should always closely examine corporate financial reports. However, because of accounting differences and other consistency problems, it can be difficult to compare the data from one company's financial report to that of another. A better bet for the beginner is to use one of the various information sources that do much of the legwork and adjustments for you. You can then refer to the corporate financial reports to doublecheck these sources and answer questions that might arise from the data they present.

The information sources presented above provide extensive information on the companies covered; while there are other sources of piecemeal information, the ones listed should present you with enough basic information to complete the simplified valuation worksheet.

Sources of Earnings Estimates

Zacks Investment Research
155 N. Wacker
Chicago, Ill. 60606
(800) 767-3771; (312) 630-9880
www.zacks.com

Institutional Brokers' Estimate System (I/B/E/S)
1 World Trade Center, 18th Fl.

New York, N.Y. 10048
(212) 437-8200
www.ibes.com

Standard & Poor's Earnings Guide
Standard & Poor's Stock Reports
Standard & Poor's Outlook
65 Broadway, 8th Floor

New York, N.Y. 10006
(800) 221-5277
www.stockinfo.standardpoor.com

Value Line Investment Survey
220 E. 42nd Street
New York, N.Y. 10017-5891
(800) 634-3583
valueline.com

Sources for Industry Statistics

Almanac of Business and Industrial Financial Ratios
Prentice Hall Business Group
Order Processing Center
P.O, Box 11071
Des Moines, Iowa 50336-1071
(800) 947-7700
www.phdirect.com
Provides financial ratios and operating factors for 181 industries classified in 16 categories. Published annually.

Barron's
Dow Jones and Co.
84 Second Ave.
Chicopee, Mass. 01020
(800) 554-0422
www.barrons.com
A listing of the Dow Jones Industry Groups is given in the Market Statistics Section.

Dun & Bradstreet Industry Norms and Key Business Ratios
One Diamond Hill Rd.
Murray Hill, N.J. 07974-0027
(908) 665-5000
www.dnb.com
Calculates industry norms of financial statement items along with 14 key business ratios on 800 types of business, one million companies private and public

nationwide grouped in 4,000 asset and geographic industry segments.

Industriscope
Media General Financial Services
P.O. Box 85333
Richmond, Va. 23293
(800) 446-7922
(804) 649-6587
ww.mgfs.com
Information on over 6,500 companies classified into 175 industry groups.

Investor's Business Daily
P.O. Box 661750
Los Angeles, Calif. 90066-8950
(800) 831-2525
Investor's Business Daily Industry Prices is presented every Tuesday and includes price changes in 197 industry indexes.
www.investors.com

RMA Annual Statement Studies
Robert Morris Associates
1 Liberty Place
1650 Market St., Suite 2300
Philadelphia, Penn. 19103
(215) 446-4170
www.rmahq.com
Composite financial data for the most recent fiscal year is provided on approximately 500 industries.

Standard & Poor's Industry Surveys
Monthly data is provided on 52 industries.
Standard & Poor's Analyst's Handbook
Reports the performance of over 70 industries as defined by the S&P subindexes.
Standard & Poor's Industry Reports
A monthly review of 52 industries.
65 Broadway, 8th Floor
New York, N.Y. 10006
(800) 221-5277
www.stockinfo.standardpoor.com

Value Line Investment Survey
220 E. 42nd Street
New York, N.Y. 10017-5891
(800) 634-3583
valueline.com
The Ratings and Reports volume (Part Three of the survey) presents composite statistics on each industry individually in various issues.

The Wall Street Journal
Dow Jones & Company
84 Second Ave.
Chicopee, Mass. 01020
(800) 568-7625
wsj.com
The Dow Jones Industry Groups is presented daily.

Sources of Information on the S&P 500 Index

Standard & Poor's Outlook
65 Broadway, 8th Floor
New York, NY 10006
(800) 221-5277
www.stockinfo.standardpoor.com

For a longer-term view of the S&P 500 index:
Standard & Poor's Security Price Index Record is published by S&P.

PROBLEMS YOU MAY ENCOUNTER

While these outside information sources are useful, it is important to understand how the information service you are using derives its figures, especially for comparative purposes. This is particularly important in the calculation of earnings per share, which is subject to some financial accounting manipulation. For instance, companies can have conservative accounting policies in which they depreciate assets relatively quickly or take large allowances for bad debt, either of which leads to greater initial expense and consequently lower earnings.

The way the information service handles accounting differences can make a big difference. As an example, Value Line does not include non-recurring gains or losses in its calculations but instead chooses to footnote those amounts. Standard & Poor's, on the other hand, chooses to include extraordinary items in its reports, which makes it possible for the two services to come up with different historical growth rates for the same company.

Dividends are subject to less accounting differences than earnings, but the information services may handle extraordinary dividends differently.

In comparing companies, the date of the fiscal year-end can also have an impact. The effect of fiscal year-end differences is sometimes magnified in times of economic turnaround or industry upheaval. Differences of only six months can have a major impact on the calculation of historical growth rates and ratios. The key is to know that such differences may exist and to keep these in mind when comparing companies.

Because of these differences, it is probably best for beginners to stick to one information source when comparing companies.

GROWTH RATES AND ESTIMATES

The simplified valuation approach requires estimates of next year's earnings and dividends per share. You can either come up with your own estimates, based on an examination of past growth and a forecast of future company and industry prospects, or use outside information sources for estimates.

Equation to Determine Growth Rate of Earnings Per Share (EPS) & Dividends Per Share (DPS)

$$(EV/BV)^{1/n} - 1.00 = g$$

Where:
- EV = Ending value (latest EPS or DPS)
- BV = Beginning value (earliest EPS or DPS)
- n = Number of yearly periods
- g = Growth rate in decimal form

Note that if you have five years of data, you will have only four yearly periods. For instance, EPS and DPS figures for 1989, 1990, 1991, 1992 and 1993 represent four yearly periods: 1989-90, 1990-91, 1991-92 and 1992-93. Also note that the formula only works when the beginning and ending figures are positive.

Equations to Estimate Next Year's EPS or DPS

$$EPS_{CY} \times (1.00 + g) = EPS_{est}$$

or

$$DPS_{CY} \times (1.00 + g) = DPS_{est}$$

Where:
- EPS_{CY} & DPS_{CY} = Current year EPS & DPS
- EPS_{est} & DPS_{est} = Next year's estimated EPS & DPS
- g = Growth rate in decimal form

Determining Growth Rate and Next Year's EPS or DPS: An Example

$$(EV/BV)^{1/n} - 1.00 = g$$

Where:
- EV = $5.00
- BV = $2.00
- n = 4
- g = Growth rate in decimal form

$$(\$5.00/\$2.00)^{1/4} - 1.00 = g$$
$$(2.50)^{1/4} - 1.00 = g$$
$$1.257 - 1.00 = g$$
$$0.257 \text{ or } 25.7\% = g$$

Estimate of Next Year's EPS or DPS:

$$\$5.00 \times (1.00 + 0.257) = EPS_{est} \text{ or } DPS_{est}$$
$$\$5.00 \times 1.257 = EPS_{est} \text{ or } DPS_{est}$$
$$\$6.28 = EPS_{est} \text{ or } DPS_{est}$$

If you wish to use the historical growth rate as a guide to future earnings and dividends, you need to determine the historical growth rate over the past five years using the historical per share data from the worksheet. The formula to calculate the growth rate is presented on the previous page.

Next year's earnings and dividends per share can then be estimated by multiplying the current year's earnings and dividends per share by 1.00 plus the growth rate. (This formula is also presented below). Of course this is a very naive forecast. You need to determine whether growth should continue at the same rate. Studying the firm, its products, and its competitive environment will help guide your decision to adjust the growth up or down.

Estimates of next year's earnings and earnings growth can also be obtained from outside sources such as Value Line, which derives its own estimates (and which also estimates dividends for the next year), or from consensus reports. In consensus reports, a large number of analysts are periodically polled and asked for their estimates of earnings per share for the next few years, along with estimates of long-term growth rates. If you do not use these estimates in your valuation, they can still provide insight to the market's perception of the firm's prospects.

INDUSTRY INFORMATION

Industry information for comparison purposes is available from a wide variety of sources. Some of these sources are expensive, so you may want to check with your local library.

Information on the overall "market" is available in many newspapers. Most sources tend to report on the price level of the Dow Jones industrials or the Dow 30. However, when performing comparative analysis of large company stocks, the standard benchmark used by analysts is the Standard & Poor's 500 index.

Appendix A

Using a Computer for Fundamental Analysis

In today's fast-paced investment world, people are increasingly turning toward computers for assistance in the investment decision process. This chapter will explore the methods of putting a computer to work locating and analyzing stocks through fundamental analysis.

Fundamental analysis refers to the process of selecting stocks based upon underlying economic trends and long-term expectations of future company performance. The crucial variable in fundamental analysis revolves around projected growth in factors such as sales, cash flow, earnings and dividends. Software for fundamental analysis is usually broken down into two categories—screening and valuation. Screening refers to the act of searching through a large universe of securities to locate a few that might hold promise and warrant further analysis. Valuation, on the other hand, refers to taking one company and applying a series of valuation models to determine if the current price can be considered fair.

FUNDAMENTAL SCREENING

Screening dictates that the search process starts with a broad universe of companies. It is not practical to enter this data by hand, so investors must either acquire the complete database and store it on their computer for screening or connecting to another computer and have it perform the screen and return only the results of the screen.

In comparing stock screening services, critical factors include: the universe of stocks supported by the database, the depth of stock information, the flexibility of screening software, the frequency of updates, distribution methods, computer system support, and price. The screening services listed vary widely in the number of stocks tracked. When contemplating a data vendor, consider the types of companies that you are trying to find. If your focus is only on larger, more established companies, then less company coverage may not be a limitation. However, if you are seeking smaller, less-followed firms, look for a service that covers a wider range of stocks.

Screening services vary in the depth of stock information they provide. Some services, such as Market Guide StockQuest, provide a fewer number of variables for each company and depend more on summary statistics such as growth rates when providing background data. Other services, such as Microsoft MoneyCentral and AAII's *Stock*

Investor, provide both summary statistics and the raw year-by-year or quarterly data behind these numbers. In considering a data service, look not only at the number of variables but also specifically at which statistics are provided. Value Line Investment Survey for Windows allows you to screen companies based upon Value Line's proprietary rankings and projected growth rates, which may be more important for some investors than a complete database. Telescan's TIP@Wallstreet with ProSearch program is the only service that combines both fundamental and technical factors for screening. Before settling on a service, obtain a listing of available screening variables to determine if the program will support those variables you find important.

SOFTWARE FLEXIBILITY

The next consideration in selecting a screening service is the flexibility of the screening software. Screening services that distribute a complete database to the user and then allow you to manipulate the data tend to offer more flexibility than strictly on-line services. For example, products such as Morningstar Principia Pro for Stocks, *Stock Investor* and Value Line Investment Survey for Windows allow users to combine existing fields to create custom variables. Look for flexibility in creating screening criteria.

When comparing programs, look for flexibility in creating the screening criteria. The Strategic Investor option on Prodigy offers a service with a rich collection of data, but lacks screening flexibility. Exporting data allows users to move information to a spreadsheet program. The better programs allow users to export company data.

DISTRIBUTION OF DATA

The method of data updating may play a role in selecting a vendor. Value Line Investment Survey for Windows allows you to update your database by both mailed disks and by downloading the data via phone lines or Internet. Other services, such as *Stock Investor*, only offer disk updates via mail. The pure on-line vendors will always require a phone call to perform a screen.

The frequency of the data updates must also be considered. On-line services typically update their database on a daily or weekly basis. If the complete database resides on your computer, then you must select a delivery schedule, which will determine the annual cost. Options vary from weekly updates to annual updates. Expect to pay anywhere from $100 to over $2,000 per year, depending upon how frequently you update and who supplies the data. For the long-term investor who is planning less frequent portfolio revisions, quarterly or monthly updating may be sufficient. For the short-term trader, weekly updating may be needed.

COMPUTERIZED INVESTING TIPS

The computer can be a very useful tool for the investor. We have provided you with a

Fundamental Screening Software: A Sampling

Disk-Based Screening

Market Guide StockQuest (Windows) Market Guide, (516) 327-2400, www.marketguide.com. $9.95/mo. (includes full Web site access)

Principia Pro for Stocks (Windows) Morningstar, (800) 735-0700, www.morningstar.com. $995/yr. weekly updates, $495/yr. monthly updates, $295/yr. quarterly updates, $95/yr. annual update.

Stock Investor (Windows) American Association of Individual Investors, (312) 280-0170, (800) 428-2244, www.aaii.com. $99/yr. quarterly updates; $150 for non-members

Value Line Investment Survey for Windows (Windows) Value Line Publishing, (800) 654-0508, valueline.com. $595/yr. monthly updates.

On-Line Screening

CoScreen on CompuServe (Mac, Windows) CompuServe, Inc., (800) 848-8990, www.compuserve.com. $24.95/month.

Prodigy Strategic Investor (Mac, Windows) Prodigy Services Company, (800) 776-3449, www.prodigy.com. $14.95/mo. core service plus Prodigy charges.

TIP@Wallstreet '98 with ProSearch (Windows) Telescan, Inc., (800) 324-8246, www.wallstreetcity.com. $349 plus $18/mo.

Internet-Based Screening

MSN MoneyCentral, Microsoft, Inc. (800) 426-9400, moneycentral.msn.com. $9.95/mo. ($6.95/mo, for MSN subscribers)

Morningstar.Net, Morningstar, Inc., (800) 735-0700, www.morningstar.net. $9.95/month or $99/year Premium Service.

Quicken.com, Intuit, Inc. (800) 446-8848, www.quicken.com. Free.

Thomson Investors Network, Thomson Financial Services, (301) 548-5800, www.thomsoninvest.net. $$34.95/year.

Wall Street City, Telescan, Inc., (281) 588-9700 www.wallstreetcity.com. Free–$149.95/year.

Yahoo! Finance, Yahoo!, Inc. (408) 731-3300, quote.yahoo.com. Free.

Zacks Analyst Watch, Zacks Investment Research, (800) 399-6659, www.zacks.com. $150/year.

list of some of the programs that are more popular with our members. Before selecting a program, keep these items in mind:

- Ask for a demo version of the product. If one is not available, get a brochure and make sure that you can return the product if you are not satisfied. Some vendors offer a full refund, others charge a restocking fee, while still others will not refund your money at all. Understand the return policy before you buy the product, not after.
- Look at the support policies of the company: Do they offer telephone support and, if so, when is it available? Some vendors charge for providing help. Some may operate a Web site or forum that you can connect to—not only to solve problems, but also to get operating tips.
- If you are purchasing via mail order, it is best to do so with a credit card. If you have problems either receiving the product or getting it to work, then you have

some recourse. The Fair Credit Billing Act gives you some power to withhold payment on items purchased if you have made a good faith effort to provide the seller with an opportunity to correct any problems.

- Most importantly, try talking to other investors. Attend a local chapter meeting or go on-line—most on-line services have investment special interest forums, which, like a BBS, allow users to read and leave electronic messages with other users.
- Check out AAII's *"Individual Investor's Guide to Computerized Investing,"* Which reviews ands rates investment software and services. Updated annually, it's available to AAII members for $19.00.

In using and selecting an investment program, keep in mind that the computer is only a tool to aid the user in the decision-making process. Just as buying a hammer will not make you a carpenter, buying a computer system and investment software will not make you a successful investor.

It is your knowledge, aided by the information gathering and processing capabilities of a computer system, that will lead to success.

4

Using the Dividend-Yield Approach to Investing

We have already laid out a basic framework for building a stock portfolio that consists of:

- Developing a list of promising candidates, with the criteria based on your return objectives, tolerance for risk, and investment philosophy. This defines your overall investment strategy;
- Performing financial statement and ratio analysis, by gathering information on and analyzing the financial condition of prospective companies;
- Performing stock valuation, which involves estimating what you feel a prospective stock is worth; and
- Making a final decision on whether to buy or not, based on a comparison of the stock's current market price to the value you have placed on the stock.

We have also discussed a simplified approach to financial statement and ratio analysis, including a worksheet to help you organize useful information. But how do you apply this simplified approach to various investment strategies? In this chapter, we'll illustrate this approach and the use of the worksheet by focusing on the dividend-yield approach to investing. Appendix B (on page 31) discusses screening on a computer database using the dividend-yield model.

DEVELOPING THE INITIAL LISTS

A dividend-yield strategy can help you find potentially undervalued stocks with low downside risk, provided the dividend is secure and expected to grow, and the firm is financially sound. This strategy will also tend to produce more income in the form of dividends, and less in the form of capital gains, than other strategies.

We have already presented sources of information for financial statement and ratio analysis. These sources provide thorough, consistent and easy-to-compare information. But it would be difficult for an investor to go through each company page by page and compare dividend yields for thousands of companies. For the beginning investor, there are other more useful sources from which you can draw your initial list of prospective candidates.

Most of the sources are inexpensive; they may also be available in your local library. Many of these sources do not present information that is sufficient or consistent (for

Drawing Up an Initial List:
Sources of Information

BusinessWeek
BusinessWeek, P.O. Box 644, Hightstown, N.J. 08520, 800/635-1200, www.businessweek.com.
Once a year in late March or early April the magazine comes out with *America's 1,000 Most Valuable Companies,* which presents one-line statistical information and ratios—including dividend yield—on each firm. It is long, but the format allows for easy comparisons.
The magazine also includes summary statistics so you can compare individual firms against the average.

Moody's Handbook of Dividend Achievers
Moody's Investors Service, Financial Information Services, 60 Madison Ave., 6th Floor, New York, NY 10010, 800/342-5647, www.moodys.com.
The book includes information on 300 companies that have increased their dividends consistently over the past 10 years. The listings include a company's dividend achiever rank, as well as the company's dividend growth rate for the latest 10-year period.
For the companies listed, the book includes the summary data pages that appear in Moody's Handbook of Common Stocks.

Standard & Poor's 500 Guide, yearly edition
Standard & Poor's MidCap 400 Guide, yearly edition
Standard & Poor's SmallCap 600 Guide, yearly edition
All are published by McGraw-Hill, P.O. Box 548, Blacklick, Ohio 43004, 800/262-4729, www.mcgraw-hill.com.
The 500 and MidCap 400 include two useful lists:
Fast-Rising Dividends: Firms whose dividend yields may not be at an absolute high, but show promise.
Higher Dividends for 10 Years: Firms that have paid higher cash dividends in each of the past 10 years and whose dividend yield is currently at least 2%, an indication of healthy finances and capable management.
These published guides include the data pages found in the S&P Stock Reports.

Standard & Poor's Earnings Guide
Standard & Poor's Corp., 65 Broadway, 8th Floor, New York, N.Y. 10006, 800/221-5277, www.stockinfo.standardpoor.com. Monthly.
Includes summary (one-line) information and focuses on earnings, but the front includes one short useful list:
Dividend Increases With Strong Coverage: These are firms that have passed a fairly rigorous screen including increasing dividends, a payout ratio that has been between 10% and 90% for each of the last five fiscal years, and an average dividend coverage (earnings divided by dividends) for five years that has been at least 1.7 (an indication of dividend safety). One advantage to this list is that it is updated monthly.

Standard & Poor's Industry Reports
This monthly review of 80 industries and some 900 stocks includes dividend yield percentages for each industry. In the back of these reports, there are one-line listings for selected companies within the industry; included in these listings are dividend yields. Thus, you can easily compare dividend yields of companies relative to their industry. The listing also provides S&P's earnings and dividend rank.

(cont'd on next page)

Value Line Investment Survey
Value Line Publishing Inc., 220 E. 42nd St., New York, N.Y. 10017-5891, 800/634-3583, valueline.com.
Part 1 Summary & Index:
The front page lists median estimated yields of all stocks. The tables in the back (see index for the page numbers) include several useful lists:
High-Yielding Stocks: This consists almost entirely of utilities, since the large number of firms in this industry causes them to dominate the list. For this reason, you would not want to concentrate solely on this list.
Highest-Yielding Non-Utility Stocks: Financial companies tend to dominate the list, but it is still useful. The listing also notes if dividend cuts are possible.

Also of Note:

One well-known newsletter that is devoted to the dividend-yield approach is Investment Quality Trends. Each newsletter looks at the dividend yield of some 350 blue-chip stocks with high ratings and strong dividend-paying histories. It is published twice monthly. $275/year

Investment Quality Trends
7440 Girard Ave., Suite 4, La Jolla, Calif. 92037
619/459-3818

instance, on a calendar-year basis) for the financial statement and ratio analysis that must be done later. In addition, several are published annually, so the information in them may become dated. However, they do provide a good starting point to narrow your search. For computer users, an initial list of candidates can be compiled by applying various screens to a database of stocks (see Appendix B).

In using these lists and screens, be careful that you do not accidentally concentrate on a specific industry; you must be particularly careful using this strategy, since utilities and, to a lesser extent, financial companies will tend to dominate many of the lists. Since the approach works best with companies paying meaningful dividends, look for dividend yields of at least 2% or more. In addition, you should decide if you want to concentrate on absolute yield (is the dividend yield high compared to all other companies?), relative yield (is it low relative to its industry or to its historical average?), or perhaps both. This will help narrow the selection. Other conditions can help narrow the selection further—a high risk ranking or rating by one of the information sources.

Once a list of candidates is established the next step is to perform an in-depth evaluation of the stocks on the list to determine the fair market value. The following example is based on published information that was available in April 1994, when the approach was applied.

BRISTOL-MYERS SQUIBB: AN EXAMPLE

Bristol-Myers Squibb offers a good example of the dividend-yield approach: In mid-April of 1994, the firm was listed in S&P's table indicating it had paid higher cash dividends in each of the past 10 calendar years, and it was listed in Value Line's table of high-yielding non-utility stocks. Its dividend yield was 5.7% as of the end of March 1994.

In mid-April of 1994, Bristol-Myers Squibb represented a fallen angel—a former growth company that had moved into a more mature, slower growth stage. It had popped up on the lists of high-yielding stocks because of concerns over both the industry and company. At that time, in comparison to the overall stock market, drug stocks had been weak performers since the beginning of 1992. Uncertainty surrounding changes to our nation's healthcare and its impact on the traditional drug manufacturers had led to devaluation of drug stocks even though the short-term profit picture had not changed. In the long term, Value Line noted at the time that the industry, long regarded as a growth vehicle, could in a "worst-case scenario" go the way of regulated utilities.

Individual company concerns for Bristol-Myers Squibb included costs associated with settling cases dealing with silicone breast implants, fewer tax credits for manufacturing operations in Puerto Rico, as well as the normal drug firm concerns involving the loss of patent protection for drug products.

Value Line was used as the source of both company and industry information on the completed valuation worksheet that follows on page 28. Entering the per share data from a source such as Value Line or S&P is a fairly straightforward process. The difficulty lies in determining the type of adjustments the data services made to provide the information. Value Line does not include nonrecurring items in its data. For 1993, Bristol-Myers had a $0.60 per share special charge for potential liabilities in connection with discontinued silicone implant operation, but this is only footnoted in the $4.40 earnings per share figure it reports for 1993. Using the reduced $3.80 figure in the valuation worksheet would change the high and low price-earnings ratios for the year, the average price-earnings ratios, the earnings per share growth rate, payout ratio, return on equity, and, ultimately, the valuation. Once you select a source for company information, it is important to stick with it for all of the data elements, unless you know how to adjust the figures to make everything comparable.

Many analysts like to use dividends to value a company because of the purity of the dividend. The reported dividend paid is exactly what was paid, while management has some latitude in reported earnings figures. They may use liberal accounting principles to report higher earnings or decide to defer or take special charges to earnings until it works to their advantage.

A Tour Through the Worksheet: Per Share Information

The first item that should strike you as you look at the price information is the change in trend that occurred between 1992 and 1993. Bristol-Myers' price peaked at just over $90 in early 1992, compared to a March 31, 1994, price of $51.50. This change coincides with weakness in the drug industry.

Next, it is important to examine the year-by-year dividend and earnings per share figures. Even though we are focusing on dividends, it is the profitability and cash generation of the firm that supports the dividend. First, examine the year-by-year figures—are they increasing, decreasing, or holding steady? Has there been a change in trend? Steady, increasing figures are best. Using the Value Line data, we see that earnings, dividends, and book value have increased every year. The five-year average growth rates for earnings and dividends have been 12.5% and 9.5%, respectively. These are strong growth rates, but both earnings and dividends show some slowdown in their growth rates in the later years. Calculating the year-by-year percentage change for earnings and dividends is an effective tool for identifying changes in trends and growth rates.

LOOKING AT THE FINANCIAL RATIOS

Since our valuation of Bristol-Myers focuses on dividend yield, the portions of the worksheet pertaining to the price-earnings ratio and earnings valuation have been grayed out.

In the dividend analysis of a firm, the consideration of the safety of the dividend is of great concern. A high current yield itself does not mean that a stock is undervalued. It may indicate that the market feels that the dividend is in jeopardy. For a high relative current dividend yield to be considered a sign of an undervalued stock, the company must be expected to continue to pay and expand the dividend both this year and for years to come.

The payout ratio (dividends per share divided by earnings per share) is particularly useful in gauging the strength of the dividend. Generally, the lower the payout ratio, the more secure the dividend. Any ratio above 50% is considered a warning sign. However, like all ratios, the payout ratio is industry-specific. Very stable industries, such as utilities, have high payout ratios, which is considered normal. A 100% payout ratio shows that a firm is paying out all of its earnings to its shareholders. Figures above 100% indicate that the payout is greater than earnings, a situation that cannot continue forever; negative ratios show that a company is paying out a dividend while losing money.

Bristol-Myers Squibb has averaged a 66% payout ratio over the last five years, a figure higher than one would generally like to see. Beyond not having enough cash to cover the dividend payment, a policy of high dividend payout may limit future growth if capital expenditures and research and development are reduced to maintain the dividend. Drug firms are not capital-intensive, but they are research-intensive. Investment in research takes many years, if ever, to pay off.

Financial leverage is another indicator of dividend safety. Heavier debt loads saddle a company with required cash outflows to bondholders, who must be paid before dividends can be paid to shareholders. A company with little debt that runs into earnings problems has the ability to borrow. For Bristol-Myers, we have used the ratio of long-term debt to equity as a measure of financial leverage. This figure was selected because comparable industry data was also available for this ratio. Bristol-Myers' ratio of 6% with a 4% five-year average is very low. This also compares favorably with the industry figures of 12% for 1993 and the industry's 15% five-year average. While the

Valuation Worksheet

Company: Bristol-Myers Squibb   **Current Price $** 51.50   **Date (** 3 / 31 / 94 **)**

Ticker BMY   **Exchange** NYSE   **Current P/E** 13.6   **Current Yield** 5.7%

Financial Statement & Ratio Analysis

	Company						Industry or Competitor		Market
Per Share Information	19 89	19 90	19 91	19 92	19 93	5-year avg	19 93	5-year avg	19 93
Price: High	58.0	68.0	89.4	90.1	67.3				
Price: Low	44.0	50.5	61.1	60.1	50.9				
Earnings per Share (EPS)	2.75	3.33	3.95	4.07	4.40	growth rate: 12.5%			
Dividends per Share (DPS)	2.00	2.12	2.40	2.76	2.88	growth rate: 9.5%			
Book Value per Share (BV)	9.67	10.34	11.15	11.62	12.10				
Financial Ratios									
Price-Earnings Ratio (P/E): Avg	18.5	17.8	19.1	18.5	13.5	17.5	NA	18.3*	21.3
High (High Price ÷ EPS)	21.1	20.4	22.6	22.1	15.3	20.3			
Low (Low Price ÷ EPS)	16.0	15.2	15.5	14.8	11.6	14.6			
Dividend Yield % (DY): Avg	4.0	3.7	3.3	3.9	5.0	4.0	NA	2.5*	2.7
High (DPS ÷ Low Price)	4.5	4.2	3.9	4.6	5.7	4.6			
Low (DPS ÷ High Price)	3.4	3.1	2.7	3.1	4.3	3.3			
Payout Ratio % (DPS ÷ EPS)	72.7	63.6	60.7	67.8	65.4	66.0	44.0	45.6	
Return on Equity % (EPS ÷ BV)	28	32	35	35	36	33	30	29	
Financial Leverage** %	5	4	2	3	6	4	12	15	

*four-year averages. Value Line did not have 1993 industry figures for those items.   Shaded areas were not needed for this valuation.
** long-term debt divided by equity.

Valuation Estimates

Model based on earnings:

Average high P/E × estimated 19 94 EPS: 20.3 × 4.70 = $95.41 (high valuation estimate)

Average low P/E × estimated 19 94 EPS: 14.6 × 4.70 = $68.62 (low valuation estimate)

Model based on dividends:

Estimated 19 94 annual DPS ÷ average low DY: 2.92 ÷ 0.033 = $88.48 (high valuation estimate)

Estimated 19 94 annual DPS ÷ average high DY: 2.92 ÷ 0.046 = $63.48 (low valuation estimate)

Use decimal form for DY. For instance 5.4% would be 0.054.

ratio of long-term debt to equity is a common ratio, it does possess some inherent weaknesses. The ratio does not consider short-term liabilities or other liabilities that are significant for Bristol-Myers. The ratio of total debt to total assets shows that liabilities are equal to about half of total assets, higher than the 34% figure for the drug industry. (This information was ascertained through AAII's *Stock Investor* program but can be calculated from a company's balance sheet as well.)

It is the dividend yield portion of the financial ratio section that is of primary importance in the dividend valuation process. Looking at year-by-year figures shows an interesting change in trend. From 1989 to 1991, Bristol-Myer's dividend yield was trending down. This was a period of tremendous performance for the drug stocks. Since then the yield has risen steadily due to an increasing dividend coupled with a stock price decline. The five-year average high and low yields are 4.6% and 3.3%, respectively, levels significantly below the current yield of 5.7%.

VALUING THE COMPANY

The bottom of the Valuation Worksheet provides valuations using the dividend-based model. Applying the model to Bristol-Myers paints an interesting picture. The first item that needs to be determined is the appropriate per share dividend for 1994. The worksheet uses Value Line's 1994 dividend estimate of $2.92, leading to a high valuation of $88.48 and low valuation of $63.48. This compares to a current (mid-April 1994) price of $51.50. But before you reach for the phone to call your broker, let's look at some of the assumptions behind the numbers.

The first area to consider is the dividend itself. The estimated 1994 figure of $2.92 represents an increase, although small, over the $2.88 dividend for 1993. If you were to expand last year's dividend by the historical growth of 9.5% you would get $3.15 [$2.88 × (1 + 0.095)], showing that $2.92 falls significantly short of the past trend. This figure even falls below Value Line's 8.5% estimate of long-term dividend growth and is the first signal of a change in trend. It is a good exercise to try different dividend estimates and see the impact on the valuation. If you think a dividend cut is possible, try the valuation with the new dividend. A halving of the $2.88 dividend to $1.44 leads to a valuation range of $31.30 to $43.64, all else being equal.

The next area to look at is the average high and low dividend yields. In considering whether the five-year averages of 3.3% and 4.6% are appropriate numbers, you need to ask whether the fundamental characteristics of the company have changed and higher levels are appropriate. If you assume the government will start to further regulate the industry and set prices, then these drug firms may become more like utilities and trade with higher expected yields, coupled with lower growth rates and lower profit margins. Under this scenario the current price seems fair. Changing the required dividend yield to 6% leads to a valuation of $48.67 using the $2.92 dividend estimate.

By changing the required dividend yield to determine the effect on valuation, you can quickly see that the stock price is even more sensitive to slight changes in yield than to changes in dividend.

CONCLUSION

Performing sensitivity analysis of this nature is a critical part of the valuation. It helps to provide you with a sense of the factors that drive a stock price and informs you of the factors to focus on when performing the valuation.

The worksheet focuses on the quantitative factors of valuation. Any final decision should also be based on a better understanding of the company, its management, and its competitive environment. This can only be accomplished by a thorough reading of the firm's financial reports, as well as the reports and summaries on the firm and its industry.

In Appendix B, we discuss the approach and some of its problems in more detail, particularly as it's used to screen a database.

Appendix B

Screening for Stocks Using a Dividend-Yield Approach

Many investors turn toward the dividend yield as a measure of value in their quest for selecting underpriced securities. A stock's dividend yield is computed by taking the indicated dividend—the most recent quarterly dividend multiplied by four—and dividing it by the share price. If a stock's price rises faster than its dividend, the dividend yield will fall, indicating that the price may have been bid up too far and may be ready for a decline. Conversely, if the dividend yield rises to a high level, the stock may be poised for an increase in price, if the dividend can be sustained.

This chapter will focus on strategies used to screen a database for high dividend-yielding stocks.

THE DIVIDEND-YIELD STRATEGY

Like all basic value-oriented techniques, the dividend-yield strategy attempts to identify investments that are out-of-favor. Contrarian techniques such as this are based on the premise that markets tend to overreact to good and bad news and push the price of a security away from its intrinsic value. Value investors hope to identify these mispriced securities through the use of a consistent set of rules called a valuation model.

Screening is the first stage in this process and it involves scanning a group of securities to find those that merit further in-depth analysis. Absolute or relative levels may be used in screening for high-yield stocks. A screen requiring an absolute level might look for a minimum dividend yield of 4% before an investment would be considered. Absolute screens can lead to passive market timing—cash levels tend to build up when investors cannot find suitable investments that meet the minimum requirement during times of market extremes. Also, screens that only look at absolute levels can be weak because they may turn up companies from a single industry that traditionally has higher dividend yields, such as utilities.

Screens based on relative levels compare the yield against a benchmark that may fluctuate, such as the current dividend yield for the S&P 500. In this case the investor does not require that the yield meet some minimum level, but instead that it maintain its historical relationship with the benchmark figure. Common screens examining relative yields include comparisons against some overall market level, industry level, historical average or even some interest rate benchmark. The screens for this chapter were performed using a historical average as the benchmark.

Investors looking to perform custom screens can use one of a number of software programs or information services that provide fundamental data on companies. (See Appendix A for information on computerized investing tools and a listing of available screening tools.)

APPLYING THE SCREENS

AAII's *Stock Investor* program was used to perform the screening.

The first filter excluded utilities, real estate investment trusts, closed-end mutual funds, and financial firms. Each of these groups has unique financial characteristics requiring that they be analyzed separately.

The next screen required that a company have five years of both price and dividend records. When screening against a historical level, remember to include a historical period that covers both the up and down periods of a stock market and economic cycle.

Selecting a time period is a balance between using one that is too short and only captures a segment of the market cycle and one that is too long and includes a time period that is no longer representative of the current company, industry, or market. Periods of between five and 10 years are most common for these types of comparisons.

Dividend analysis is geared toward established firms that are past their explosive growth and capital-intensive stage. To help filter out companies paying just token dividends, a minimum dividend yield of 2% was specified.

Beyond a minimum level of dividends, we screened for companies that have paid a dividend for each of the last five years and never reduced their dividend. Dividend levels are set by the board of directors based on consideration of the current company, industry, and economic conditions. Because dividend cuts are tantamount to an announcement that the firm is financially distressed, dividends are set at levels that the company should be able to afford throughout the economic cycle.

The next filter required that the company's current dividend yield be higher than its five-year average dividend yield. This filter seeks out companies whose dividends have increased faster than increases in share price, or whose current share price has dipped recently.

While it might seem that screening should be over with this last filter, the security of the dividend must be examined before a company can be considered a buy. A high dividend yield may be a signal that the market expects the dividend to be cut shortly and has pushed down the price accordingly. A high relative dividend yield is a buy signal only if the dividend level is expected to be sustained and hopefully increased.

Measures exist that help to identify the safety of the dividend. The payout ratio is perhaps the most common of these and is calculated by dividing the dividend per share by earnings per share. Generally the lower the number, the more secure the dividend. Any ratio above 50% is considered a warning flag. However, for some industries, such as utilities, ratios around 80% are common. The current payout ratio for the Dow Jones

Definitions of Screens

The following is a short description of the screens and terms used in the table.

Dividend Yield: Indicated dividend divided by current price. Provides a relative valuation measure when compared against historical average dividend yield.

Five-Year Average Yield: Average company dividend yield during the last five years.

Indicated Dividend: Expected per share dividend payment for the next year.

Dividend Growth Rate: Annual dividend growth rate in dividends per share over the last five years. An indication of the past company strength and dividend payment policy.

Cash Dividends Paid Since: The number of consecutive years that a cash dividend has been paid. An indication of the stability of the company's past dividend payment policy.

Payout Ratio: Dividends per share for the last 12 months divided by earnings per share for the last 12 months. Provides an indication of the safety of the dividend. Figures between 0% and 50% are considered safe. Figures ranging between 50% and 100% are considered early warning flags. Negative values and values above 100% are considered red flags for a dividend cut if the levels persist. Beyond examining a single year, look for trends.

EPS Growth Rate: Annual growth rate in earnings per share over the past five years.

52-Week Relative Strength: The price performance of a stock during the last year relative to the performance of the overall stock market. A figure of 100% indicates the stock had the same percentage price performance as the market. A figure of 105% indicates that the stock outperformed the market by 5%.

utility group is 82%, versus 55% for the Dow Jones industrial group. A 100% payout ratio indicates that a company is paying out all of its earnings in the form of dividends. A negative payout ratio indicates that a firm is paying a dividend even though earnings are negative. Firms cannot afford to pay out more than they earn in the long term. For the final criterion we required a payout ratio between 0% and 50%, leaving 86 companies.

To highlight a cross section of stocks, along with any differences due to company size, the stocks were divided up into three groups based upon market capitalization. The top 15 dividend-yielding stocks for each group are listed. Market capitalization is determined by multiplying the number of shares outstanding times a firm's stock price. The largest firms have a market capitalization above $1.5 billion dollars, the middle capitalization firms range in size between $250 million and $1.5 billion, and the small capitalization firms are those below $250 million in market capitalization.

THE RESULTS

The screening used data that was current as of March 31, 1994. The three groups, while similar in fundamentals differ slightly. The mid-cap stocks have the highest dividend

Top Dividend Yielders

company (exchange)	div yield (%)	5-yr avg yield (%)	indic'd div ($)	div grth rate (%)	cash div paid since	payout ratio (%)	EPS grth rate (%)	52-wk rel strgth (%)	description
Large Cap (above $1.5 billion)									
Clorox Co.* (NY)	3.6	3.2	1.80	11.9	1968	47.2	8.0	94	Mfrs, mkts non-durable consumer prod
Cooper Indus* (NY)	3.6	2.4	1.32	7.3	1947	47.3	2.3	73	Compression, drill equip; electric, electron prod
Times Mirror* (NY)	3.5	3.3	1.08	4.1	1892	43.9	−35.7	89	Newspaper, book pub; newsprint; info serv; TV
Quaker Oats* (NY)	3.4	2.3	2.12	12.9	1906	45.6	11.3	89	Produces groceries, cereals, snacks, pet food
Brown-Forman B* (NY)	3.3	2.5	2.84	14.1	1960	46.2	2.3	97	Produces distilled spirits & wines
Dresser Indus* (NY)	3.2	2.7	0.68	7.5	1948	31.7	−6.6	98	Supplier of prods & serv to oil, gas devlp cos
Schering-Plough* (NY)	3.2	2.2	1.80	18.2	1957	41.1	19.3	92	Mfrs drugs & beauty aids
Norfolk Southern* (NY)	3.0	2.8	1.92	9.3	1901	47.2	2.9	97	Holding co: Norfolk; Western & Southern rail
General Electric* (NY)	2.9	2.7	2.88	11.3	1899	41.6	8.6	106	Power systems; consumer & indus'l prod
CPC Int'l* (NY)	2.9	2.4	1.36	10.3	1920	42.7	8.7	103	Branded grocery products business
Honeywell Inc.* (NY)	2.9	2.3	0.96	12.2	1928	37.9	33.0	98	Mfrs heat & air condition'g control
Abbott Labs* (NY)	2.9	1.5	0.76	18.9	1926	39.1	15.0	100	Pharmaceuticals; hospital, laboratory prod
Union Pacific* (NY)	2.8	2.4	1.60	7.8	1900	44.0	6.0	88	Transportion; energy & natural resources
Gerber Products* (NY)	2.8	2.0	0.86	21.3	1941	46.5	14.7	95	Consumer prod for infant care; trucking
Johnson & Johnson* (NY)	2.8	1.5	1.04	16.7	1905	36.9	14.5	89	Healthcare, pharm'cal, industrial prod
Mid Cap ($250 million to $1.5 billion)									
Pacific Telecom (NM)	5.7	4.5	1.32	8.1	1976	43.9	−22.8	94	Telephone communication serv
Goodrich, B. F.* (NY)	5.2	4.8	2.20	6.3	1938	47.0	−20.3	82	Mfrs, sells chemical intermed & polymeric prod
Handleman Co.* (NY)	4.0	2.6	0.44	4.0	1963	44.0	0.8	69	Sell/distrib prerecorded music & books
GATX Corp. (NY)	3.6	3.4	1.50	9.6	1919	46.8	−24.5	115	Mfrs railcars, specific steel & indus'l equip
Ennis Business Forms (NY)	3.6	2.9	0.56	13.1	1973	47.9	6.8	87	Mfrs business forms & paper items
Longs Drug Stores* (NY)	3.4	2.6	1.12	6.6	1961	46.5	−1.6	89	Oper drugstore chain
EG&G Inc.* (NY)	3.4	2.0	0.56	13.0	1965	36.9	7.9	69	Mfrs, mkts electronic instruments
Amer. Business Prod (NY)	3.3	3.1	0.80	9.6	1941	48.1	5.3	86	Business forms & supplies

Top Dividend Yielders (continued)

company (exchange)	div yield (%)	5-yr avg yield (%)	indic'd div ($)	div grth rate (%)	cash div paid since	payout ratio (%)	EPS grth rate (%)	52-wk rel strgth (%)	description
Crawford & Co. B (NY)	3.3	1.8	0.50	14.1	1965	41.5	7.6	66	Insurance claims adjusters
Block Drugs Co. (NM)	3.2	1.6	1.04	15.8	1971	35.7	9.5	64	Mfr denture, dental care products; drugs
Kimball Int'l B (NM)	3.1	2.6	0.84	12.2	1954	45.5	−2.7	93	Mfrs pianos, organs, office & home furn
Gallagher (Arthur J.) (NY)	3.1	2.3	0.88	8.2	1985	34.7	9.2	77	Insurance broker; risk management
Giant Food A* (AM)	3.1	2.1	0.70	15.7	1960	45.8	−4.3	85	Supermarket chain
Universal Foods (NY)	3.0	2.3	0.92	13.5	1934	40.1	7.7	82	Mfrs, produces foods & beverages
Mercantile Stores* (NY)	2.7	2.6	1.02	6.9	1940	43.4	−11.9	103	Dept stores; beauty salons; shopping ctrs

Small Cap (below $250 million)

company (exchange)	div yield (%)	5-yr avg yield (%)	indic'd div ($)	div grth rate (%)	cash div paid since	payout ratio (%)	EPS grth rate (%)	52-wk rel strgth (%)	description
Nash Finch Co. (NM)	4.4	3.6	0.72	2.2	1965	49.3	2.6	81	Distrib wholesale, retail supermkt prod
Marsh Supermkts A (NM)	4.2	2.7	0.44	5.9	1960	45.8	3.5	71	Oper supermrkts & convenience stores
Dibrell Brothers (NM)	3.8	2.2	0.72	20.4	1925	34.5	26.8	62	Process, mkts tobacco
United Stationers (NM)	3.3	3.2	0.40	1.3	1972	34.8	−7.9	62	Distrib wholesale office prod to retailers
MMI Medical (NM)	3.2	2.6	0.16	2.4	1988	24.6	−4.9	75	Medical diagnostic imaging serv
Stepan Co. (AM)	3.2	2.3	0.84	11.4	1967	41.3	−5.5	77	Produces basic & intermediate chemicals
Sealright Inc. (NM)	3.2	1.5	0.46	28.6	1986	45.0	3.5	65	Mfr, mkts round paperboard & plastic containers
Hako Minuteman (NM)	3.1	3.0	0.32	8.8	1988	42.4	−4.1	117	Makes, distrib floor & carpet care equip
Fay's Inc. (NY)	3.1	2.2	0.20	7.9	1975	40.0	1.4	84	Oper chain of retail drug stores
Flamemaster Corp (NM)	3.1	2.1	0.12	18.9	1989	42.9	15.6	83	Makes flame retardant & heat resistant prod
Zero Corp (NY)	3.0	2.9	0.40	4.1	1974	49.4	−7.7	89	Mfrs electron pack'g & special enclosures
Analysts Int'l Corp. (NM)	2.7	2.6	0.48	9.6	1988	36.2	12.0	84	Furnishes computer programming serv
Super Food Services (NY)	2.7	2.3	0.36	4.1	1971	40.9	−12.8	124	Wholesale food distrib & support serv
Insteel Indus (NY)	2.7	2.2	0.24	8.3	1986	31.4	−7.0	77	Mfsr welded wire prod
General Binding (NM)	2.7	1.6	0.40	18.1	1975	42.1	3.3	86	Mfrs business machines & supplies

*S&P 500 stock
Exchanges: NY= New York Stock Exchange; AM= American Stock
Exchange; NM= Nasdaq National Market

Source: Stock Investor/Media General; data
as of March 31, 1994.

yield among the three groups. It was also surprising to find a number of S&P 500 stocks among these mid-cap securities. (Firms in the S&P 500 index are identified with an asterisk.) This, along with the 52-week relative strength measure points to a collection of companies that have stumbled slightly, and the relative performance of their stock prices indicates this. The 52-week relative strength measures the relative stock price performance versus the market as a whole. Figures above 100% indicate that a stock has outperformed the market, while figures below 100% indicate underperformance. The vast majority of the companies that passed the screens have underperformed the market over the last year. The small caps, however, showed the weakest performance, both fundamentally in terms of earnings growth and technically in terms of price strength.

Screening for relative high dividend yield is based upon the time-honored rule of buying low and selling high. Examining a stock's dividend yield provides a useful framework to identify potential candidates.

To succeed at this strategy, you need to develop a set of tools to not only identify which stocks have relatively high dividend yields but also which of these stocks have the strength to bounce back.

5

A Basic Strategy for Growth Stock Investing

A growth approach to investing can help you find stocks with the potential for significant price appreciation, provided the firm is able to meet and exceed its growth expectations and you don't overpay for growth. This strategy produces very little return in the form of dividends and can be volatile because of the large role that expectations play in the pricing of these stocks.

COMPANY CHARACTERISTICS

Growth companies expand at a rate above that of the overall economy. Practically speaking, however, the minimum benchmark for being classified as a growth stock is at least a 10% annual growth rate in earnings per share, with many investors requiring a 20% annual growth rate. To maintain growth rates this high over any extended period, capital spending is required, and for this reason growth stocks tend to retain most of their earnings, paying little or no cash dividends.

Promising growth stocks attract a great deal of attention, and therefore prices tend to be bid up with high anticipation. High expectations relative to current levels of earnings lead to high price-earnings ratios, and it is not uncommon to see highly touted growth stocks with price-earnings ratios two to four times that of the market.

As long as the firm maintains its earnings per share momentum and exceeds the growth expectations of the market, its stock price can be expected to increase by quite a bit. However, a small deviation from market expectations during a quarterly earnings announcement can send the price flying in either direction. Thus, while growth stocks have the potential for high returns, they are also high risk.

THE INITIAL LIST

The first step in the basic framework, of course, is drawing up an initial list of promising candidates for further analysis. A growth approach focuses initially on companies that consistently have had above-average earnings growth over the past few years.

For the beginning investor, there are several sources from which you can draw your initial list. Most of these sources are inexpensive and may also be available at your local library. Keep in mind that these sources are useful primarily for the initial list—many of them do not present information that is sufficient or consistent for the financial state-

Drawing Up an Initial List:
Sources of Information for the Growth Approach

BusinessWeek
BusinessWeek, P.O. Box 644, Hightstown, N.J. 08520, 800/635-1200, www.businessweek.com.
Once a year in late May the magazine comes out with an issue that includes The Best Small
Companies, a ranking of small firms (annual sales between $10 million and $150 million) based on
three-year results in sales growth, earnings growth and return on invested capital. The listing includes
a short description of each firm.

Standard & Poor's 500 Guide, yearly edition
Standard & Poor's MidCap 400 Guide, yearly edition
Standard & Poor's SmallCap 600 Guide, yearly edition
All are published by McGraw-Hill, P.O. Box 548, Blacklick, Ohio 43004, 800/262-4729, www.mcgraw-
hill.com. $19.95 each for the 500 and MidCap 400 Guides, $27.95 for the SmallCap 600 Guide
The 500 and MidCap 400 Guides include two useful lists:
Companies With Five Consecutive Years of Earnings Increase: Firms that have recorded rising earnings
per share for five consecutive years, have a minimum 10% earnings per share growth rate based on
trailing 12-month earnings, have estimated 1993 earnings per share at least 10% above those
reported for 1992, pay dividends, and have S&P earnings and dividend rankings of A– or better.
Rapid Growth Stocks: Firms that have shown strong and consistent earnings growth.
These annual guides include the full-page data pages found in the S&P Stock Reports; since they are
published annually, the data can be dated.

Standard & Poor's Earnings Guide
Standard & Poor's Corp., 65 Broadway, 8th Floor, New York, N.Y. 10006, 800/221-5277,
www.stockinfo.standardpoor.com. Monthly.
Includes summary (one-line) information and focuses on earnings and earnings growth estimates. The
front includes two short useful lists:
Rapid Growth Stocks: These are firms that have been selected by S&P for superior earnings growth,
with actual and estimated five-year annual earnings growth rates of at least 10%.
Standard & Poor's A+ Ranked Stocks: These firms carry high S&P rankings, have projected five-year
earnings growth rates of at least 12%, are estimated to show earnings gains of at least 12% for each
of the next two years, and have price-earnings ratios on estimated 1995 earnings of under 20.
One advantage to these lists is that they are updated monthly.

Value Line Investment Survey
Value Line Publishing Inc., 220 E. 42nd St., New York, N.Y. 10017-5891, 800/634-3583,
valueline.com.
Part 1 Summary & Index:
The tables in the back (see index for the page numbers) include this useful list:
High Growth Stocks: This consists of firms with average growth rates of 13% or more over the last 10
years and estimated 13% or more growth in the next five years.

ment and ratio analysis that must be done later. In addition, several are published annually, so the information in them may become dated—a particular concern for growth investors, since quarterly earnings reports can produce unexpected surprises. However, they do provide a starting point to narrow your search.

For computer users, an initial list of candidates can be compiled by applying various screens to a database of stocks. Appendix C (on page 45) discusses screens based on the growth approach.

In using these lists and screens, be careful that you do not accidentally concentrate on a specific industry. In addition, cyclical companies may turn up on growth lists at certain times if they are in an upswing in their cycle. For this reason, make sure that you examine earnings growth over longer time periods covering at least one economic cycle to make sure you are focusing on true growth companies. Requiring consistently rising earnings each year can also help identify more stable growth companies. Other conditions can help narrow the selection further—for instance, eliminating companies with outrageous price-earnings ratios.

Once a list of candidates is established, the next step is to perform an in-depth evaluation of the stocks on the list to determine the fair market value.

The following example is based on published information that was available in May of 1994, when the approach was applied.

Toys "R" Us: An Example

Toys "R" Us offers a good example of a growth stock examination: In mid-May of 1994, the firm was listed in the S&P Earnings Guide's list of rapid growth stocks, indicating it had actual and estimated five-year annual earnings growth rates of at least 10%. It also made Value Line's high growth stock list, indicating an average growth rate of 13% or more over the last 10 years and an estimated 13% or more growth rate in the next five years.

In mid-May of 1994, Toys "R" Us represented a growth company that continued its expansion despite its large market capitalization. It had done so first by outmatching its competition, and then by expanding its markets. The toy retailer had more recently ventured into children's clothing (through its Kids "R" Us stores), mail catalog sales, action figure and video software products, and foreign operations.

It was the latter area—foreign markets—that was at that time coming under increasing scrutiny in analysts' projections. In any growth company, a major concern is how the company can continue to expand. Toys "R" Us at that time dominated the retail U.S. toy market, with subsequently less room to expand, and the retail market was not a growth industry; the focus, therefore, was into expanding their product lines or opening more stores overseas.

The completed valuation worksheet for Toys "R" Us is shown on the next page. Value Line was used as the source of both company and industry information.

Entering the per share data from an information source is relatively straightforward, but it is important to stick to the same source for company information, since reporting

Valuation Worksheet

Company: Toys "R" Us   Current Price $ 34.62   Date (4 / 29 / 94)

Ticker TOY   Exchange NYSE   Current P/E 21.2   Current Yield 0%

Financial Statement & Ratio Analysis

Per Share Information	19 89	19 90	19 91	19 92	19 93	5-year avg	Industry or Competitor 1993	5-year avg	Market 19 93
Price: High	26.80	35.00	36.00	41.00	42.90				
Price: Low	16.00	19.90	22.00	30.40	32.40				
Earnings per Share (EPS)	1.09	1.11	1.15	1.47	1.65	growth rate: 10.9%			
Dividends per Share (DPS)	0.00	0.00	0.00	0.00	0.00	growth rate: na			
Book Value per Share (BV)	5.95	7.11	8.39	9.85	11.60				

Financial Ratios

	19 89	19 90	19 91	19 92	19 93	5-year avg	Industry or Competitor 1993	5-year avg	Market 19 93
Price-Earnings Ratio (P/E): Avg	19.6	24.7	25.2	24.3	22.8	23.3	19.0	17.9	21.3
High (High Price ÷ EPS)	24.6	31.5	31.3	27.9	26.0	28.3			
Low (Low Price ÷ EPS)	14.7	17.9	19.1	20.7	19.6	18.4			
Dividend Yield % (DY): Avg	0.0	0.0	0.0	0.0	0.0	0.0	1.0	1.1	2.7
High (DPS ÷ Low Price)	0.0	0.0	0.0	0.0	0.0	0.0			
Low (DPS ÷ High Price)	0.0	0.0	0.0	0.0	0.0	0.0			
Payout Ratio % (DPS ÷ EPS)	0.0	0.0	0.0	0.0	0.0	0.0	22.0	21.0	
Return on Equity % (EPS ÷ BV)	18.3	15.6	13.7	14.9	14.2	15.4	15.0	15.7	
Financial Leverage* %	10.1	9.5	16.1	23.2	19.5	15.6	30.4	34.1	

*long-term debt divided by equity.   *Figures in gray type were not needed for this valuation.*

Valuation Estimates

Model based on earnings:

Average high P/E × estimated 19 94 EPS: 28.3 × $1.83 = $51.79 (high valuation estimate)

Average low P/E × estimated 19 94 EPS: 18.4 × $1.83 = $33.67 (low valuation estimate)

Model based on dividends:

Estimated 19___ annual DPS ÷ average low DY: _____ ÷ _____ = _____ (high valuation estimate)

Estimated 19___ annual DPS ÷ average high DY: _____ ÷ _____ = _____ (low valuation estimate)

Use decimal form for DY. For instance 5.4% would be 0.054.

services make different adjustments to the data they provide. However, one potential source of confusion may come when trying to determine the actual years covered by the data reporting source. For example, Toy's "R" Us has a fiscal year-end of January 31, which means that most of the activity for the firm will have taken place in the previous year. Value Line reports data for 1993 based on the January 31, 1994, fiscal year-end report. Standard & Poor's, on the other hand, reports 1993 data based on the January 31, 1993, fiscal year-end—1992 data in Value Line's report.

A Tour Through the Worksheet: Per Share Information

The first item that may strike you is that the stock price that is "current" on the worksheet is nearly 20% below its all-time highs in 1993—double the market's decline from its high over the same time.

Toys "R" Us reacted in classical growth stock fashion: Its price took a fall after the first of the year because it only met—and failed to exceed—expected predictions for a strong Christmas season. Underlying the strong but expected domestic performance was lower than expected foreign sales. Prices had not yet recovered from the post-holiday drop.

Next, it is important to examine the year-by-year earnings per share figures. Are they steadily increasing, or has there been a change in trend? Earnings clearly increased, but the biggest increase occurred in 1992 when earnings shot up 27.8%. Calculating the year-by-year percentage change for earnings is an effective tool for identifying changes in trends and growth rates.

The Value Line data also shows an increase in book value every year.

Looking at the Financial Ratios

Toys "R" Us pays no dividend and so the portions of the worksheet pertaining to dividend yield and dividend valuation appear in gray typeface. However, that doesn't mean that the company's dividend policy can't generate some useful insight.

Growth firms generally pay no dividends because they want to use capital for expansion. Toys "R" Us in the spring of 1994 paid no dividends, but it had recently announced a buy-back of $1 billion worth of shares over the next few years. At a minimum this is a sign that the company is generating more cash than it feels it needs for future expansion. As companies first move to buy back shares and then pay cash dividends, they are indicating that new projects are not offering the same return potential to the company as once was the case. The move could be one sign that Toys "R" Us may be reaching a more mature stage—it may be turning into more of a mature company rather than a growth firm. In such a situation, the price-earnings ratio would contract and a given level of earnings would support a lower price.

In a growth approach, the historical earnings growth rate provides one guide to future growth. But equally important are market expectations concerning future growth rates. Examining the price-earnings ratios are useful to judge market expectations concerning the future growth of the firm.

At 21.2, the current (mid-May 1994) price-earnings ratio of Toys "R" Us is edging toward the lower end of its historical range. It is still above the industry average, and close to the market's 1993 ratio—which is low for a growth stock. Traditionally the price-earnings ratio of a growth stock trades above that of the market and the Toys "R" Us ratio has traditionally been about 20% above the market's. While a low price-earnings ratio can be a sign of an undervalued stock, it can also be a sign that the market has lowered its expectations for the firm—it may no longer view the company as a true growth stock. It is worthwhile to consider whether the market may be correct in its assessment.

The 1993 return on equity for Toys "R" Us was below both the long-term average and the industry average. The return on equity measures how well the firm is being run on both an operational and financial basis. To boost return on equity a company must increase the profit margin on goods being sold, make better use of its assets, or increase the level of financial leverage. While the ratio is close to industry norms, the slide in return on equity for Toys "R" Us is surprising in light of the increase in financial leverage. An examination of the profit margin over this time shows an overall decline; battling the competition does have its costs, as does expansion. However, the profit margin has shown an increase lately.

VALUING THE COMPANY

The bottom of the Valuation Worksheet provides valuations using the earnings-based model. Applying the model to Toys "R" Us paints an interesting picture.

The first item that needs to be determined is the appropriate per share earnings figure for 1994. The worksheet uses an estimate based on the five-year earnings growth rate of 10.9% and the most recently reported earnings per share [1.65 × (1 + 0.109)], leading to a high valuation of $51.79 and a low valuation of $33.67. This compares to a current price of $34.62. Sounds enticing, but let's look at some of the assumptions.

Is the growth rate reasonable? Actually the growth rate used here (10.9%) is somewhat below the rates estimated by other analysts. For instance, Value Line estimates a higher growth rate of 17.5%, while the S&P Earnings Guide projects a growth rate of 18%. Using a higher growth rate would, of course, raise the valuations somewhat.

Of greater concern, however, are the high and low price-earnings ratios based on historical averages. These averages are based on a time period when the company was clearly a growth stock. But as we have seen, there are reasons to question whether the company can continue to be considered a growth firm; the market right now may be raising questions about this.

If Toys "R" Us is valued as a mature stock, its price-earnings ratio would on average parallel the market's. Currently (mid-May, 1994), the market's price-earnings ratio is 20.6; using that in the model would produce a valuation of $37.70 based on the worksheet's 1994 earnings per share estimate; using Value Line's higher 1994 earnings per share estimate would produce a valuation of around $41.

CONCLUSION

Examining different assumptions is a critical part of the valuation, and will help you isolate some of the major factors that are affecting a stock's price.

While the worksheet examines quantitative factors, it is clear that many subjective factors go into the equation. To judge these factors, it is necessary to go beyond the statistics. Any final decision should be based on a better understanding of the company, its management, and its competitive environment. This can only be accomplished by a thorough reading of the firm's financial reports, as well as the reports and summaries on the firm and its industry.

Appendix C

Screening Stocks With High Growth Potential

The mention of growth investing brings a sparkle to many an investor's eye. Looking for rapidly growing firms in hot industries seems much sexier than picking through the value plays that other investors have cast off. But searching for growth stocks is like all investment techniques—it has its ups and downs. The allure of buying into a stock with the potential for a tenfold increase in price must be balanced with the potential for substantial price declines if the firm fails to meet the market's growth expectations.

This chapter focuses on strategies used to screen a database for growth stocks.

Screening for Growth

Screening can be used as a first step in identifying growth stock prospects. Screening is the process of applying a set of criteria to a set of stocks to filter out those companies that merit more detailed examination. Readers with access to computers can use a number of software programs or Internet services to screen for growth stocks. AAII's *Stock Investor* program was used to perform the screening.

While there are many ways to measure company growth, most investors focus on earnings growth, with an emphasis on a high and expanding rate of growth. A common first screen for growth stocks is to specify an absolute minimum growth level. A minimum annual growth rate of 15% in earnings from continuous operations over the last five years was the first screen applied in our example. While 15% may not seem very restrictive, it will knock out most of the cyclical firms just coming out of the recession. In selecting a time period for historical analysis, the economic environment should be kept in mind. True growth companies are expanding throughout the economic cycle.

Screening based upon earnings requires a careful analysis of a firm's reports, which can highlight how the growth was achieved. Was the growth due to acquisition or internal expansion? Did currency translation impact on earnings? How are same store sales? To help buffer the impact of extraordinary items on earnings, earnings from continuing operations were used throughout. Looking at sales growth will also provide a confirmation of how earnings were achieved.

SECONDARY GROWTH SCREENS

The next filter applied examined year-to-year earnings per share changes from continuing operations. In screening for growth companies it is important to examine the year-to-year figures for steady and increasing earnings. A screen requiring increased earnings for each of the last five years was specified. If you wish to be more stringent in your screening, you might require an increase in the year-to-year growth rate for each of the last five years. This more stringent screen focuses on the momentum of earnings.

Investors examining growth stocks look toward any signs that a trend in growth may be broken. Quarterly earnings are closely examined and deviations from the expected norm are quickly rewarded or punished. The seasonality of sales and earnings for most firms, however, do not allow investors to compare one quarter to the preceding quarter in a meaningful manner. To deal with seasonality, it is best to compare one quarterly figure to the same quarter one year prior. A decrease from the same quarter one year ago is a warning flag that merits investigation. In our screening process, higher quarterly earnings than the same quarter one year ago for each of the last four quarters was required.

Beyond examining overall growth or momentum, many investors examine how a company compares to its industry peers. The ability to expand within an industry group may point to a firm that has a competitive edge. Therefore, our final growth screen specified the company's earnings growth to be above that of its industry's average.

One other screen we applied excluded financial firms because of the non-compatibility of the financial statements.

VIEWING THE RESULTS

The screening used data that was current as of April 30, 1994. To highlight a cross section of companies, the firms passing the screens were divided up into groups based upon market capitalization. The top 15 large-cap and mid-cap companies ranked by historical growth in earnings from continuing operations are shown. Also shown are 13 Shadow Stock companies that passed all the screening requirements. (Shadow Stocks are defined by AAII as stocks of non-financial companies that are small, with low institutional interest, and that have had positive annual earnings for the two previous years.)

Our screen focused on historical performance, but growth stock investors really focus on expected performance. Looking at market consensus forecast figures helps to provide an indication of the expectations surrounding the valuation. It is the company's ability to meet and, more importantly, exceed these expectations that leads to great gains. For example, Cisco Systems had the second highest historical earnings growth of the large-cap stocks. Just after the screen was performed for this table, Cisco came out with a quarterly earnings announcement that met the market's consensus estimate. However, in prior years Cisco had consistently exceeded the consensus estimates. The

Stocks With High Earnings Growth

company (exchange)	EPS growth rate hist'l avg (%)	EPS growth rate I/B/E/S est (%)	EPS last 12 mo ($)	EPS current fiscal yr forecast ($)	P/E ratio trailing 12 mo (X)	P/E ratio fiscal yr est (X)	hist'l sales grth rate (%)	52-wk rel strength (%)	description
Large Cap (above $1.5 billion)									
U.S. Healthcare (NM)	180.0	17.5	2.00	2.25	18.8	16.7	31.2	114	Health maintenance organization
Cisco Systems (NM)	140.6	35.0	0.92	1.22	32.9	24.8	120.0	138	Mfrs computer network products
Parametric Tech (NM)	96.8	40.0	0.95	1.12	30.0	25.4	96.2	97	Devlps, mkts integrated software prod
United Healthcare (NY)	67.2	28.0	1.25	1.65	33.2	25.2	58.4	145	HMO administra'n serv on contract basis
EMC Corp. (NY)	62.7	30.0	0.77	0.96	23.2	18.6	56.0	212	Designs, mkts enhancem't prod for computers
Amer Power Convers'n (NM)	57.8	35.0	0.60	0.75	37.1	29.7	73.5	154	Devlp, mkts power supply products
Cabletron Systems (NY)	57.7	25.0	4.20	5.30	24.5	19.4	66.2	111	Hardware & software prod supporting LANs
CUC International (NY)	52.1	28.0	0.77	0.98	38.2	30.0	28.8	134	Member-based consumer services
Intel Corp (NM)	49.5	18.0	5.38	5.95	11.3	10.3	29.5	121	Designs, mfrs semicond components, systems
BMC Software (NM)	47.4	25.0	3.10	4.00	19.4	15.0	41.0	112	Devlps standard systems software products
Microsoft Corp (NM)	47.3	25.0	3.72	3.92	24.9	23.6	47.0	102	Designs, mfrs, mkts software packages
Blockbuster Entertain (NY)	39.9	25.0	1.18	1.35	23.0	20.1	53.4	144	Owning and licensing videotape stores
Linear Technology (NM)	38.4	25.0	1.36	1.49	34.9	31.9	23.6	180	Designs, mfrs linear integrated circuits
Sysco Corp (NY)	37.7	16.5	1.16	1.21	22.4	21.5	10.0	98	Distrib consumer foods & food serv
Home Depot (NY)	37.4	30.0	1.01	1.32	41.6	31.8	37.5	93	Retail building material stores
S&P 500	**−1.1**	**8.0**	**21.98**	**30.42**	**20.5**	**14.8**	**na**	**na**	
Medium Cap ($250 million to $1.5 billion)									
Vencor Inc (NY)	93.8	26.5	1.37	1.60	23.8	20.4	51.4	126	Acute-care servs to complex patients
Westcott Commun'ns (NM)	77.1	35.0	0.55	0.74	30.0	22.3	44.7	99	Prod training, educational programs
CML Group (NY)	75.1	20.0	1.26	1.30	10.7	10.4	28.8	50	Specialty retail
Snyder Oil Corp. (NY)	64.2	15.0	0.80	0.59	24.4	33.1	41.1	103	Oil & gas producing prop/gas processing
Owens & Minor (NY)	62.2	16.0	0.94	1.05	24.7	22.1	10.0	142	Wholesale drug, hospital & surgical supplies
Xilinx Inc (NM)	61.3	30.0	1.71	2.30	32.5	24.1	55.6	164	Mfrs semiconductors, system develop software

company (exchange)	EPS growth rate		EPS last 12 mo ($)	EPS current fiscal yr forecast ($)	P/E ratio		hist'l sales grth rate (%)	52-wk rel strength (%)	description
	hist'l avg (%)	I/B/E/S est (%)			trailing 12 mo (X)	fiscal yr est (X)			
Invacare Corp. (NM)	59.8	16.0	1.54	1.75	17.4	15.3	18.4	104	Designs, mfrs durable medical equip
Tech Data Corp. (NM)	59.0	25.0	0.83	1.05	21.5	17.0	44.9	146	Distrib computer-related prods
Briggs & Stratton (NY)	53.1	10.0	6.14	6.22	13.7	13.5	6.8	126	Manufactures air-cooled engines & auto locks
KCS Energy Inc (NY)	49.5	na	1.20	2.41	20.2	10.1	38.8	118	Holding co.: propane distrib, oil & gas serv
Applebee's Internat'l (NM)	47.2	30.0	0.45	0.60	47.8	35.8	27.0	189	Franchises/opers national restaurant chain
Bowne & Co. (AM)	45.3	na	2.20	2.18	10.5	10.6	15.1	112	Finance & corporation printing
Horizon Healthcare (NY)	44.5	25.0	0.94	0.90	24.9	26.0	20.6	174	Opers long-term care facilities
Oakwood Homes (NY)	44.4	18.0	1.40	1.45	15.3	14.7	31.9	110	Mfrs mobile homes, oper mobile home parks
Progress Software (NM)	44.4	28.0	2.02	2.40	22.0	18.5	44.8	109	Devlp, support integrated application software
S&P MidCap 400	na	na	7.97	8.75	21.7	19.7	na	na	

Shadow Stocks (small firms with low institutional interest)

company (exchange)	hist'l avg (%)	I/B/E/S est (%)	EPS last 12 mo ($)	EPS current fiscal yr forecast ($)	trailing 12 mo (X)	fiscal yr est (X)	hist'l sales grth rate (%)	52-wk rel strength (%)	description
Ashworth Inc* (NM)	144.9	35.0	0.36	0.47	30.6	23.4	116.1	133	Mfrs golf apparel
Homecare Mgmt Inc (NM)	95.7	na	0.54	0.54	30.8	30.8	80.3	153	Home care service to elderly
Methode Elec B (NM)	59.7	17.5	0.77	0.85	22.7	20.6	8.9	113	Mfrs electro component devices
Marten Transport (NM)	55.5	15.0	1.58	1.62	10.8	10.5	11.2	123	Long-haul truckload carrier
Gates/F.A. Distrib (NM)	55.4	30.0	1.20	1.27	16.5	15.6	32.9	140	Distribs microcomputers & periph
Rotech Medical Corp (NM)	45.9	na	0.85	0.98	23.2	20.2	39.4	158	Mkts, distribs home healthcare prod
Medical Tech Sys (NM)	39.7	na	0.68	na	12.3	na	66.1	89	Mfrs, sells nursing home equip
Turf Paradise Inc (NS)	31.6	na	0.67	na	16.8	na	−0.7	163	Oper horse racing track in Arizona
Cosmetic Center B (NM)	30.8	20.0	0.93	1.02	18.2	16.5	14.0	141	Retail & distrib'n of cosmetics
Volunteer Capital (NY)	22.6	35.0	0.93	0.45	12.6	26.1	0.8	138	Own, franchisor of fast food restaurants
Diodes Inc (AM)	20.2	na	0.42	na	21.7	na	7.5	491	Semiconductor devices
BGS Systems (NM)	19.8	na	2.23	2.55	9.3	8.1	13.9	53	Design, devlp software prod
Reflectone Inc (NM)	19.8	na	0.86	na	9.9	na	10.4	93	Flight simulators & training devices

Formerly Charter Golf Inc.
Exchanges: NY = New York Stock Exchange; AM = American Stock Exchange; NM = Nasdaq National Market; NS = Nasdaq Small Cap.

Sources: Stock Investor/Media General data as of April 30, 1994; I/B/E/S data as of May 13, 1994.

market greeted the earnings announcement with a big price decline for Cisco and many of its technology competitors.

The price-earnings ratios for stocks on our list tended to be above the market average, as would be expected for companies with above-average prospects. To better judge price-earnings ratios, many analysts look at price compared to forecasted earnings. For the S&P 500, this brought its high trailing price-earnings ratio of 20.5 back to a more reasonable price-earnings ratio fiscal year estimate of 14.8.

The 52-week relative strength figures point to a collection of companies that have largely outperformed the market—quite a contrast to the value-based stocks presented in Appendix B (see pages 34 and 35). The relative strength figures near 50% for a few of these companies, however, reveal the volatility of this group.

Investing in growth stocks can be an extremely rewarding experience. Success, however, requires careful analysis and constant monitoring of the portfolio.

Definitions of Screens and Terms

EPS Growth Rate—Historical Average: Annual growth in earnings per share from continuing operations over the last five fiscal years. A measure of how successful the firm has been in generating the bottom line, net profit.

EPS Growth Rate—I/B/E/S Est.: The median growth rate in earnings per share from continuing operations over the next five years that is being forecasted by analysts as reported by I/B/E/S, a firm that surveys analysts (212/437-8200; www.ibes.com). An indication of the consensus in earnings growth expectations for the firm.

EPS Last 12 Mo.: Earnings from continuing operations for the most recent 12 months divided by the number of common shares outstanding.

EPS Current Fiscal Yr. Forecast: Earnings from continuing operations for the current fiscal year of the company that is being forecasted by analysts as reported by I/B/E/S.

Price-Earnings Ratio—Trailing 12 Mo.: Market price per share divided by most recent 12

months' earnings per share from continuing operations. A measure of the market's expectations regarding the firm's earnings growth and risk. Firms with very high price-earnings ratios are being valued by the market on the basis of high expected growth potential.

Price-Earnings Ratio—Fiscal Yr. Est.: Market price per share divided by earnings per share from continuing operations that is being forecasted by analysts as reported by I/B/E/S, a firm that surveys analysts.

Historical Sales Growth Rate: Annual growth in total sales per share over the last five fiscal years for the firm. Used to provide a confirmation of the quality of the historical earnings per share growth rate.

52-Week Relative Strength: The price performance of a stock during the last year relative to the performance of the overall stock market. A figure of 100% indicates the stock had the same percentage price performance as the market. A figure of 105% indicates that the stock outperformed the market by 5%.

Investing in Utilities for Income and Growth

Most investors look to utility stocks primarily for yield, with some expectation of share price increase. While utilities in the past have been viewed as staid, the industry is facing stiffer challenges from non-regulated sources, a tougher regulatory environment, and deregulation in certain areas.

Although growth prospects are limited, they do exist. Growth from a total return viewpoint—including both capital gains and dividends—usually emerges when a utility is positioned in an area with significant population growth, when it has deftly sidestepped the pitfalls of new plant construction, when it has diversified into non-regulated businesses that may prosper, or even during potential takeover situations, which are increasingly common in the utility sector.

COMPANY CHARACTERISTICS

The average utility is still purchased for the dividend flow, which is usually two to three times the dividend yield of the average industrial stock. This yield component makes them competitive with bonds, and as such they are affected by changes in interest rates. In addition, the industry is highly leveraged, and interest costs consequently play a large role in the earnings equation. The combination of these two factors make utilities highly interest-rate sensitive: When interest rates fall, utilities rise in price, and when rates rise, utility prices suffer.

While the utility sector generally has lower risks, calamities do occur beyond the rare nuclear plant meltdown—construction delays and cost overruns, adverse regulatory decisions, failures in non-regulated businesses, unusual weather conditions affecting demand, and economic busts in single-industry dominated areas. Dividend cuts or suspensions on a stock bought primarily for dividend yield can be devastating.

Utility stocks are often recommended as defensive investments in times of economic uncertainty. The reasoning: If the economy turns down, the demand for electricity, gas, and water may decline somewhat for industrial users, but overall demand will not suffer significantly. Couple that with the likely decline in interest rates in an economic slowdown, and utility stocks can be expected to buck the trend of declining stock prices.

Conversely, interest rates tend to rise during expansions, and utility stocks tend to decline in this stage.

Many utilities offer dividend reinvestment programs, which provide investors with a low-transaction-cost method of reinvesting dividend payments; some plans also allow additional cash investments. The existence of a dividend reinvestment plan is an added investor benefit, but stock selection decisions should be based on fundamental merits.

THE INITIAL LIST

For the beginning investor, there are several sources from which you can draw your initial list of promising utilities. Most of these sources are inexpensive, and may also be available in your local library. Keep in mind that these sources are useful primarily for the initial list. In addition, several are published annually, so the information may become dated. However, they do provide a starting point to narrow your search.

For computer users, an initial list of candidates can be compiled by applying various screens to a database of stocks. Appendix D (on page 59) discusses screens that are useful in analyzing utilities.

In using these lists and screens when searching for utilities, keep in mind that you are concentrating on an industry, but one that has several components: natural gas distributors, water companies, and electric utilities. Diversifying among these components—as well as geographically—would reduce some of the risks specific to the particular industry sector.

For most investors, utilities are primarily income plays. That means focusing not only on dividend yield but also consistent dividend payments. A high ranking for earnings and dividend growth and stability, or a high rating for dividend safety by one of the information sources can narrow the selection.

Once a list of candidates is established, the next step is to perform an in-depth evaluation. The following example is based on published information that was available in June of 1994 when the approach was applied.

SCANA CORP.: AN EXAMPLE

SCANA Corp. offers a good example of how the approach can be applied to utilities. In June of 1994, the firm appeared in Value Line's High-Yielding Stocks list (based on next year's estimated dividends per share) while at the same time ranking above average for relative safety. It also appeared in Moody's Handbook of Dividend Achievers, indicating it had increased its dividend consistently over the past 10 years. It had a high S&P earnings and dividend ranking (A–) and was rated above average in appreciation potential by S&P (reported in Industry Reports).

SCANA Corp. is the holding company for South Carolina Electric & Gas Co., which provides electricity (74% of its revenues) and gas (26% of revenues) to central and southern South Carolina. Its fuels for generating electricity are coal (71%, according to Value Line), nuclear power (22%), and hydroelectric power (7%).

As with many utilities at the time, earnings growth projections were not stellar, due to little room for growth in its consumer base and a few uncertainties on the regulatory

Drawing Up an Initial List: Sources of Information

Moody's Handbook of Dividend Achievers, yearly edition
Moody's Investors Service, 99 Church St., New York, N.Y. 10007, 800/342-5647, www.moodys.com. $19.95
The book includes information on over 300 companies that have increased their dividends consistently over the past 10 years, many of which are utilities. The listings include a company's dividend achiever rank, as well as the company's dividend growth rate for the latest 10-year period. The book also provides full-page data summaries on each dividend achiever.

Standard & Poor's 500 Guide, yearly edition
Standard & Poor's MidCap 400 Guide, yearly edition
Standard & Poor's SmallCap 600 Guide, yearly edition
All are published by McGraw-Hill, P.O. Box 548, Blacklick, Ohio 43004, 800/262-4729, www.mcgraw-hill.com. $24.95 each.
The 500 and MidCap 400 Guides include this list:
Higher Dividends for Ten Years: Firms that have paid higher cash dividends in each of the past 10 years and whose current dividend yield is at least 2%, indicating healthy finances and capable management.
These annual guides include the full-page data pages found in the S&P Stock Reports; since they are published annually, the data can be dated.

Standard & Poor's Industry Reports
Standard & Poor's Corp., 65 Broadway, 8th Floor, New York, N.Y. 10006, 800/221-5277, www.stockinfo.standardpoor.com. $241.00
This monthly review of 80 industries and some 900 stocks; utilities are divided into: electric utilities, natural gas, and water suppliers. In the back of the industry reports are one-line listings for the selected companies within each industry, allowing for comparison of the various firms listed relative to others in the same industry. For each stock, the S&P's earnings and dividend rank and S&P's evaluation of its investment potential (using their Stock Appreciation Ranking System) are included, which allow easy selection and comparison.

Value Line Investment Survey
Value Line Publishing Inc., 220 E. 42nd St., New York, N.Y. 10017-5891, 800/634-3583, valueline.com. $525.00
Part 1 Summary & Index:
The tables in the back (see index for the page numbers) include several useful lists from which to draw prospects:
Conservative Stocks: Stocks ranked high by Value Line for relative safety.
High Yielding Stocks: This consists almost entirely of utilities, ranked by yield, based on estimated year-ahead dividends per share.
Highest Estimated 3- to 5-Year Dividend Relative to Current Price: These rankings are based on the projected dividends per share in three to five years, divided by recent price.
Widest Discount from Book Value and Lowest P/Es: Both of these lists may contain a smattering of utilities that may be good prospects.

Also of Note:
Standard & Poor's Industry Surveys, Standard & Poor's Corp., 65 Broadway, New York, N.Y. 10006, 800/221-5277. Provides surveys on 21 industry groups that are updated periodically.

front. On the other hand, SCANA's expansion into non-regulated activities brought some promise to the earnings picture.

On the following page is the completed valuation worksheet for SCANA. Value Line was used as the source of both company and industry information.

Entering the per share data from an information source is relatively straightforward, but it is important to stick to the same source for company information, since reporting services make different adjustments to the data they provide.

PER SHARE INFORMATION

The first item that may strike you is that the May 31, 1994, stock price had fallen nearly 18% recently from its all-time highs in 1993. This price drop reflected the overall decline that utilities faced due to rising interest rates at the time. On the other hand, SCANA's drop was much less than the industry's as a whole.

Next, it is important to examine the year-by-year earnings per share figures. Are they steadily increasing, or has there been a change in trend? SCANA's earnings only slowly increased, except for 1992, when they dropped due primarily to increases in certain expenses. While 1993's earnings appear much higher, Value Line reports that earnings were inflated due to a particularly hot summer. As a result, Value Line's projected earnings for 1994 are slightly below 1993 earnings, assuming normal weather conditions.

Dividends, on the other hand, increased only modestly every year. The five-year average growth rate is 2.7%, or slightly below the current rate of inflation.

In examining a utility, it is useful to compare the average growth rate in earnings relative to the average growth rate in dividends. This provides a measure of the potential stability and growth of the dividend, since over the long term, dividends cannot continue to grow faster than earnings. While both the growth rates for SCANA are modest, the five-year average earnings growth rate is above the five-year average dividend growth rate.

LOOKING AT THE FINANCIAL RATIOS

Dividend concerns tend to drive the prices of utility stocks. Not surprisingly, SCANA's dividend yield was high, at 6.4% as of May 31, 1994, compared to the market's yield of 2.9% at that time. However, it is not high relative to the industry's 7% yield at that time (for the Dow utility average), and it is near its historical low of 6.2%. Higher than average dividend yields are not necessarily an indication of a good value (high dividends at a low price); rather, they may indicate that the market feels the dividend is in jeopardy.

The payout ratio (dividends per share divided by earnings per share) also helps gauge the strength of the dividend: The lower the payout ratio, the better, implying that the dividend payment is more secure. A 100% payout ratio shows that a firm is paying out all of its earnings to its shareholders. The payout ratio for SCANA, 73.3% in 1993, is near the industry average of 79%.

Valuation Worksheet*

Company: SCANA Corp. **Current Price $** 43.88 **Date (** 5 / 31 / 94 **)**

Ticker SCG **Exchange** NYSE **Current P/E** 11.6 **Current Yield** 6.4%

Financial Statement & Ratio Analysis

Per Share Information	19 89	19 90	19 91	19 92	19 93	5-year avg	19 93	5-year avg	19 93
	Company						Industry or Competitor		Market
Price: High	35.80	35.80	44.30	44.80	52.30				
Price: Low	29.60	30.30	33.50	38.60	40.10				
Earnings per Share (EPS)	3.04	3.31	3.37	2.84	3.72	growth rate: 5.2%			
Dividends per Share (DPS)	2.46	2.52	2.62	2.68	2.74	growth rate: 2.7%			
Book Value per Share (BV)	22.79	24.56	25.23	26.46	28.59				
Financial Ratios									
Price-Earnings Ratio (P/E): Avg	10.8	10.0	11.5	14.7	12.4	11.9	14.2	12.6*	21.3
High (High Price ÷ EPS)	11.8	10.8	13.1	15.8	14.1	13.1			
Low (Low Price ÷ EPS)	9.7	9.2	9.9	13.6	10.8	10.6			
Dividend Yield % (DY): Avg	7.6	7.6	6.9	6.4	6.0	6.9	5.5	6.3*	2.7
High (DPS ÷ Low Price)	8.3	8.3	7.8	6.9	6.8	7.6			
Low (DPS ÷ High Price)	6.9	7.0	5.9	6.0	5.2	6.2			
Payout Ratio % (DPS ÷ EPS)	80.9	76.1	77.7	94.4	73.3	80.5	79	82*	
Return on Equity % (EPS ÷ BV)	13.3	13.5	13.4	10.7	13.0	12.8	11.6	11.2*	
Financial Leverage %	49.8	46.2	50.1	49.2	50.2	49.1	49.0	49.9*	

*1990 through 1993

Valuation Estimates

Model based on earnings:

Average high P/E × estimated 19 94 EPS: 13.1 × 3.60 = $47.16 (high valuation estimate)
Average low P/E × estimated 19 94 EPS: 10.6 × 3.60 = $38.16 (low valuation estimate)

Model based on dividends:

Estimated 19 94 annual DPS ÷ average low DY: 2.82 ÷ 0.062 = $45.48 (high valuation estimate)
Estimated 19 94 annual DPS ÷ average high DY: 2.82 ÷ 0.076 = $37.11 (low valuation estimate)
Use decimal form for DY. For instance 5.4% would be 0.054.
*Worksheet figures do not reflect a 2-for-1 stock split in 1995.

Financial leverage is another indication of dividend safety. Heavy debt loads saddle a company with required cash outflows to bondholders, who must be paid before dividends can be paid to shareholders. Utilities tend to be heavily leveraged, and interest costs have a major impact on a utility's bottom line earnings. SCANA Corp.'s use of financial leverage, while high at 50.2% in 1993, is average for the industry, at 49% in 1993.

The 1993 return on equity of 13% for SCANA Corp. was close to its long-term average and slightly above the industry's 11.6%. The return on equity measures how well the firm is being run on both an operational and financial basis. For regulated utilities, return on equity is a function of the allowable rate of return, cost structure, and use of financial leverage. SCANA's use of financial leverage is relatively unchanged. It appears that the firm has instead been able to increase its competitive edge.

VALUING THE COMPANY

The bottom of the valuation worksheet provides valuations using both the earnings-based model and dividend-based model.

The first item that needs to be determined is the appropriate per share earnings figure for 1994. The worksheet uses the Value Line estimate of $3.60. This produces a lower figure than an estimate based on the five-year earnings growth rate of 5.2% and the most recently reported earnings per share of $3.72. The five-year growth rate is based on 1993 earnings that, according to Value Line, were high due to extraordinary weather conditions; the Value Line estimate for 1994 earnings per share is more conservative, and in line with other analysts' estimates as reported by S&P. Using the Value Line estimates leads to a high valuation estimate of $47.16 and a low valuation estimate of $38.16.

Determining the appropriate dividends per share figure for 1994 is somewhat easier since dividends tend to be more stable. Using the five-year growth rate to project next year's dividend produces a $2.81 estimate [$2.74 × (1 + 0.027)], almost identical to Value Line's projection of $2.82. Using the Value Line figure in the dividend model produces a high valuation estimate of $45.48 and a low valuation estimate of $37.11.

The May 31, 1994, price of SCANA Corp. was $43.88, which falls in between the two valuations—neither a screaming buy, nor an obvious sell. But remember, this is a utility.

SCANA offers a dividend reinvestment plan, and allows investors to buy initial shares directly from the firm.

CONCLUSION

The current level of the dividend, the expected growth and the safety of the dividend payment, and the overall interest rate environment drive the prices of utility stocks. Examining these features is critical in your evaluation. The valuation models will most likely not turn up any startling results. But what you are looking for is high income with some growth potential at a fair price.

While the worksheet examines quantitative factors, it is clear that many subjective factors go into the equation. To judge these factors, it is necessary to go beyond the statistics. Any final decision should be based on a better understanding of the company, its management, and its competitive and regulatory environment. The box below provides a summary of these factors. However, a full understanding can only be accomplished by a thorough reading of the firm's financial reports, as well as the reports and summaries on the firm and its industry.

Some Factors to Consider When Evaluating a Utility

Company factors	Questions to ask:

Type of Utility
   Electric
   Gas
   Water
	Is the utility diversified or of one particular type? Diversification among various types of utilities helps reduce some of the risks of investing in this sector. Are there changes in the competitive or regulatory environment that may affect a particular type of utility?

Customer Base
   Residential
   Commercial
   Industrial
	Does any one predominate? Is the population growing, with the potential for an expanding residential base? Are there external factors (for instance, extraordinary weather conditions, or an economic downturn) that may affect industrial or commercial use?

Power Source
   Nuclear
   Coal
   Gas
   Oil
   Hydroelectric
	Does any source of power predominate? What factors affect the cost of the power sources? Items to look for include the age of a nuclear plant; type of coal used and where it is obtained; the price and supply of oil; weather patterns that may affect hydroelectric power.

Other Factors
   Non-regulated businesses
   Management
   Technology
	Is the utility moving into non-regulated businesses, and if so, how risky and how promising are they? Is there potential for reducing operating costs by better management and/or new technology?

External factors	Questions to ask:

Economic
   Interest rate outlook
   Business cycle
	What is the outlook for interest rates? Rising rates affect the cost of borrowing, a major cost to utilities. What stage in the cycle is the economy? A sagging economy can affect industrial and commercial use.

Regulatory
   Federal
   State
	What laws and regulations may affect the industry? On the national level, federal laws concerning the environment may affect some utilities more than others. At the state level, where utility rates are controlled, what is the regulatory mood?

Appendix D

Screening Utility Stocks

Utility stocks have traditionally been a mainstay in the portfolio of a conservative investor looking for the benefit of high dividend payouts that keep up with inflation over time. But what was once thought of as a stodgy, safe investment has gone through some difficult times.

This chapter covers screens for high-yielding utility stocks and discusses some of the concerns in determining if they merit further analysis.

Many investors turn toward the dividend yield as a measure of value in their quest for selecting underpriced securities. A stock's dividend yield is computed by taking the indicated dividend—the most recent quarterly dividend multiplied by four—and dividing it by the share price. Like all basic value-oriented techniques, the dividend yield strategy attempts to identify investments that are incorrectly out of favor. Contrarian techniques such as this are based on the premise that markets tend to overreact to information—both to the upside and downside—and push the price of a security away from its true intrinsic value. The danger with a strategy such as this is that a dividend cut will occur.

The screening for the high-yielding utility dividend stocks began with a database of over 8,000 companies, trusts, and closed-end funds found in *Stock Investor*. The first filter excluded non-utility firms leaving a group of 220 stocks.

We then screened for utilities that have paid a dividend for each of the last five years and never reduced their dividend. Dividend levels are set by the board of directors based upon considerations of the current company, industry, and economic condition. Because dividend cuts are tantamount to an announcement that the firm is financially distressed, dividends are set at base levels that the company should be able to afford throughout the economic cycle. The filter requiring five years of steady or increasing dividends cut the number of stocks down to 124.

The next requirement was that earnings per share from continuing operations be positive for the last 12 months. This screen cut out just two utilities. The last screen required that the firm's dividend yield be higher than its respective narrow industry group average. The final screen brought the number of utilities down to 54.

To show a cross section of the stocks and highlight any differences that company size might have, the stocks were divided up into three groups based upon market capitalization. The top 15 dividend-yielding stocks for each group are also listed. Note however that only 12 large-cap stocks made the listing.

The screening used data that was current as of May 31, 1994. The impact of market

High-Yielding Utility Stocks

company (exchange)	div yield (%)	indic'd div ($)	hist div grth rate (%)	EPS growth rate hist avg (%)	EPS growth rate I/B/E/S est (%)	payout ratio trailing EPS (%)	payout ratio I/B/E/S est (%)	S&P earn'gs & div ranking (%)	description
Large Cap (above $1.5 billion)									
Texas Utilities (NY)	9.3	3.08	1.3	(21.8)	3.0	240.6	112.0	B+	Electric utility holding co
Houston Industries (NY)	9.3	3.00	0.3	(0.9)	3.5	91.5	91.5	B+	Oper electric utility co
Potomac Electric Power (NY)	8.5	1.66	2.9	(2.5)	2.5	84.6	87.4	A–	Electric utility in greater Wash, DC area
American Electric Power (NY)	8.3	2.40	0.4	(12.3)	3.0	118.2	85.7	B+	Electric utility co for Ohio, Ky, Va, Ind, WV
Central & South West (NY)	7.7	1.70	5.7	(3.9)	3.9	105.1	82.9	A–	Electric utilities holding co
Northeast Utilities (NY)	7.7	1.76	0.0	(3.8)	4.0	92.6	85.9	B	Electric utility holding co in Conn, Mass
Allegheny Power System (NY)	7.7	1.64	1.3	0.3	2.8	83.7	85.0	A–	Electric utility holding co in Penn, WV, Md, Va
Penn. Power & Light (NY)	7.5	1.67	3.7	0.5	3.0	79.2	79.5	A–	Electric utility in Penn
Florida Progress (NY)	7.4	1.98	3.2	(2.4)	3.0	88.4	84.3	A–	Electric utility holding co
Union Electric Co (NY)	7.1	2.38	3.7	1.5	3.0	87.1	79.9	A–	Provides elec in Mo, Ill, Iowa; gas in Ill & Mo
Carolina Power & Light (NY)	7.0	1.70	3.5	0.0	3.5	79.4	73.9	A–	Electric utility co serving NC & SC
New England Electric (NY)	6.5	2.30	1.9	5.6	3.0	69.8	73.5	A–	Electric utility holding co
Average	**7.8**	**2.11**	**2.3**	**(3.3)**	**3.2**	**101.7**	**85.1**		
Medium Cap ($250 million to $1.5 billion)									
Puget Sound Pwr, Light (NY)	10.1	1.84	1.0	1.6	2.0	100.5	96.8	B+	Electric util in Washington state
Southwestern Pub. Serv. (NY)	9.0	2.20	0.2	(0.2)	2.0	92.4	93.6	A–	Electric utility in Texas, Oka, NM
Nevada Power (NY)	8.7	1.60	1.0	(0.7)	2.9	98.2	91.4	B+	Electric utility serv in Las Vegas
United Illuminating (NY)	8.0	2.76	3.3	25.0	4.0	102.7	81.2	B	Electric utility serv in Conn
Santa Fe Pacific Pipeline (NY)	7.8	2.80	12.0	(8.7)	4.0	126.1	77.1	NR	Petroleum pipeline svcs
Minnesota Power & Light (NY)	7.7	2.02	2.7	(6.7)	3.0	109.8	87.8	A–	Provides electric utility serv
Buckeye Partners L.P. (NY)	7.4	2.70	1.5	4.0	4.0	72.8	75.0	NR	Transportation of petroleum products
IPALCO Enterprises (NY)	7.2	2.12	4.4	(5.8)	4.0	101.0	80.0	B+	Electric utility serv to Indianapolis
Hawaiian Electric Indus (NY)	7.2	2.32	2.6	(6.1)	3.5	122.3	89.2	A–	Electric utility holding co

company (exchange)	div yield (%)	indic'd div ($)	hist div grth rate (%)	EPS growth rate		payout ratio		S&P earn'gs & div ranking (%)	description
				hist avg (%)	I/B/E/S est (%)	trailing EPS (%)	I/B/E/S est (%)		
Kansas City Power & Light (NY)	7.1	1.48	4.0	0.0	3.1	93.6	87.1	B+	Electric utility in Kansas City area
ONEOK Inc (NY)	6.8	1.12	21.9	2.6	6.5	83.2	94.1	B	Distrib natural gas; expl/ prod oil & gas
UGI Corp (NY)	6.6	1.38	4.7	(10.8)	7.0	106.3	98.6	B	Operates gas & elec utility
United Water Resources (NY)	6.6	0.92	2.3	(5.3)	na	83.6	89.3	B+	Operates water utility in NJ
Peoples Energy (NY)	6.5	1.80	3.2	(3.1)	5.0	79.3	81.8	B+	Operates gas utility in Chicago
New Jersey Resources (NY)	6.3	1.52	4.8	(0.5)	5.0	86.9	82.6	B	Real estate; distrib, devlp natural gas
Average	**7.5**	**1.91**	**4.6**	**(1.0)**	**4.0**	**97.2**	**87.1**		
Small Cap (below $250 million)									
Bangor Hydro-Electric (NY)	9.6	1.32	5.1	(1.4)	na	377.1	na	B	Supplies electric serv to eastern Maine
Green Mountain Power (NY)	7.6	2.12	2.0	(1.7)	2.7	100.0	94.2	A–	Electricity supplier in Vermont
Pennsylvania Enterprises (NY)	7.5	2.20	0.0	(9.2)	na	125.7	100.0	B	Natural gas and water supplier
Empire District Electric (NY)	7.4	1.28	3.2	(5.7)	7.0	113.3	102.4	A–	Electric utility serv to Ozark area
South Jersey Industries (NY)	7.4	1.44	1.6	(1.7)	3.5	92.9	90.6	B+	Distributes natural gas
E'Town Corp (NY)	7.3	2.04	0.8	12.3	na	78.3	86.8	B+	Water utility in NJ
NUI Corp (NY)	7.2	1.60	0.5	5.2	4.0	111.9	97.0	B	Gas utility holding co in NJ, Fla
Maine Public Serv (AM)	7.2	1.84	3.2	4.2	na	56.9	na	B	Electric utility service provider
IWC Resources (NM)	6.9	1.40	0.4	8.2	na	106.1	90.3	NR	Water utility
United Cities Gas (NM)	6.5	1.00	3.0	(5.9)	5.0	79.4	80.0	B+	Distrib natural gas & propane
Consumers Water (NM)	6.5	1.16	2.3	10.8	4.0	168.1	95.1	B+	Ownership & mgmt of water utility
Southern Calif. Water (NY)	6.5	1.20	3.4	4.7	na	76.4	75.5	A–	Water utility
Connecticut Water Serv (NM)	6.5	1.64	1.3	4.0	na	81.2	78.8	B+	Holding company for Connecticut Water Co
Chesapeake Utilities (NY)	6.5	0.88	0.9	0.0	na	66.7	76.5	B	Natural gas distrib co
Philadelphia Suburban (NY)	6.3	1.12	3.3	4.9	4.0	85.0	86.2	B+	Public water serv
Average	**7.1**	**1.48**	**2.1**	**1.9**	**4.3**	**114.6**	**88.7**		

NR = not rated; na = not available
Exchanges: NY = New York Stock Exchange; AM = American Stock Exchange; NM = Nasdaq National Market; NS = Nasdaq Small Cap

Sources: Stock Investor/Media General; I/B/E/S; and S&P Stock Guide. All data as of May 31, 1994.

capitalization can be seen by the types of utilities that make up each segment. Traditionally, a substantial capital investment was required to produce electricity in an economical and stable fashion. All of the large-cap stocks are fundamentally electric utilities. The medium-cap stocks are a mix of electric and gas utilities, with a single water utility. The small-cap stock section is the most varied, with a large number of water utilities mixed in with electric and gas utilities.

Definitions of Screens and Terms

Dividend Yield: Indicated annual dividend divided by market price.

Indicated Annual Dividend: Most recent quarterly dividend multiplied by four. Indicates the annual cash flow per share that is expected over the next year.

Historical Dividend Growth Rate: The compound annual growth rate in dividends over the last five years. An indication of past company strengths and dividend payment policy. Can be compared with the rate of inflation to provide an indication of real growth in dividends.

EPS Growth Rate—Historical Average: Annual growth in earnings per share from continuing operations over the last five fiscal years. A measure of how successful the firm has been in generating the bottom line, net profit. Used here in comparison with the annual growth rate in dividends per share: Over the long term, dividends cannot grow faster than earnings.

EPS Growth Rate—I/B/E/S Estimate: The median growth rate in earnings per share from continuing operations over the next five years that is being forecasted by analysts as reported by I/B/E/S, a firm that surveys analysts (212/437-8200; www.ibes.com). An indication of the consensus in earnings growth expectations for the firm. This helps to indicate the potential to increase dividends in the future.

Payout Ratio—Trailing EPS: Dividends per share for the last 12 months divided by earnings per share for the last 12 months. Provides an indication of the safety of the dividend. Figures between 0% and 80% are considered safe for utilities. Figures ranging between 80% and 100% are early warning flags. Negative values and values above 100% are considered red flags for a dividend cut if the levels persist. Beyond examining a single year, look for trends.

Payout Ratio—I/B/E/S Estimate: Indicated dividend divided by earnings estimate as reported by I/B/E/S, a firm that surveys analysts, for current fiscal year. Provides an indication of the safety of future dividends.

S&P Earnings and Dividend Ranking: Growth and stability of earnings and dividends of one company relative to others, based on 10 years of earnings and dividend data, and ranked by Standard & Poor's.

A+	Highest
A	High
A–	Above Average
B+	Average
B	Below Average
B–	Lower
C	Lowest
D	In Reorganization

The yields of these utilities are high by any measure. All of these utilities have yields above the 5.7% average for the S&P utilities index at the time of the screen.

Yields this high look very attractive on the surface, but before a company can be considered promising, the security of the dividend must be examined. A high dividend yield indicates that the market feels that the future of the dividend is risky. A high dividend yield is promising only if the dividend level can be sustained and hopefully increased.

The historical dividend growth rate indicates that, even though all the stocks have maintained their dividends, the five-year dividend growth rate has been anemic, except for two medium-cap gas stocks. The dividend growth rate should exceed the rate of inflation to provide real dividend growth and stock price increases over time.

Looking at earnings growth helps to show the company's ability to increase dividends. Over time, dividends cannot grow faster than earnings. The historical earnings growth for over half of these utilities has been negative. While the estimates for future earnings of all the firms were positive, the levels of growth were low. Looking at future earnings prospects helps to determine the ability of the company to meet and expand the dividend.

Beyond earnings growth, the payout ratio is the most common measure of a firm's ability to sustain dividends. It is calculated by dividing the dividend per share by earnings per share. Generally the lower the number, the more secure the dividend. Traditionally for utilities, any ratio above 80% is considered a warning flag. The payout ratio for the Dow Jones utility group at that time was 82% versus 55% for the Dow Jones industrial group.

The payout ratios for these utilities are at the high end. Beyond looking at payouts based upon historical earnings, it is helpful to compare the current indicated dividend to the expected earnings per share, which is shown in the I/B/E/S payout ratio estimate. It is the expectations of future earnings that drive dividend setting policies.

The final figure presented is the S&P earnings and dividends ranking. A B+ is considered average, and while the majority of the utilities ranked as average or above, a number of these utilities fell below the average ranking. None fell into the two highest groups.

The utility market is becoming more complex. The results of the screen showed that a number of high-yielding utilities existed at that time and could reward the investor with a significant current income plus the potential for capital gain. The risks for this group are above average, and a great deal of careful analysis must be performed before any utility should be added to your utility portfolio.

Investing in Low P/E Stocks

A strategy that focuses on low price-earnings ratios is a value approach that can help you find stocks with hidden or undiscovered potential for significant price appreciation, provided you are correct in your assessment of the firm and the market eventually comes to agree with you. This strategy can produce more income in the form of dividends than other strategies, and it tends to be less volatile; on the other hand, it requires patience, since it can take time for the market to recognize value.

STOCK CHARACTERISTICS

Value investors are searching for undervalued companies—firms whose stocks are selling at prices below their true per share "worth." How do you measure worth? One measure focuses on the amount of earnings that will be generated by the firm in the future on each share of stock.

A stock's price-earnings ratio—its share price divided by the most recent 12-months' earnings per share—embodies the market's expectations of a company's ability to generate earnings. If the market has low earnings growth expectations for the firm or it views earnings as uncertain, it will not be willing to pay as much per share as it would for a firm with high earnings growth expectations. The share price on these firms is bid down, and the result is a low price-earnings ratio.

That doesn't mean that all stocks with low price-earnings ratios have little or no growth potential. While many do, indeed, deserve their low ratios, value investors hope to identify firms that the market has misjudged—firms that really do have potential and whose stocks are undervalued either out of neglect or due to a market overreaction to bad news.

Stocks that have low price-earnings ratios may be in out-of-favor industries, or in cyclical industries that are in their down phase. In addition, they may have other traits indicating their out-of-favor status, including high dividend yields (if the firm pays dividends) and low price-to-book-value ratios (book value per share is total assets less all liabilities divided by shares outstanding and is a measure of the firm's net worth per share).

These stocks also tend to be less volatile, since bad news is already reflected in their relatively low prices. On the other hand, it may take considerable time for the market to recognize value, and of course, there is the risk that the market was right in its assessment after all.

Drawing Up an Initial List: Sources of Information

Standard & Poor's Earnings Guide
Standard & Poor's Corp., 65 Broadway, 8th Floor, New York, N.Y. 10006, 800/221-5277, www.stockinfo.standardpoor.com.
(Monthly) Includes summary (one-line) information and focuses on earnings and earnings growth estimates. The front includes short useful lists, some of which appear each month and some of which appear periodically.
Strong EPS & Dividends to P/E Ratio: This is a value measure that compares earnings growth (earnings growth and the dividend yield) to the price-earnings ratio. Inclusion is limited to firms that pay dividends and have five years of positive earnings.
Potential Value Plays: These firms are selling at a discount to net tangible book value, a maximum price-earnings ratio (based on next year's earnings estimates) of 15 and a projected 10% increase in earnings.
Low Rank, Low Price, Estimates Up: These firms have low rankings, indicating a history of disappointing earnings and dividend payments, and all sufferred losses in the previous year. However, they are expected to be profitable in the current year and show strong earnings gains by the next year.
Forward Growth and Low P/Es: These firms are selling at price-earnings ratios of less than 12 based on next year's earnings estimates, but earnings are expected to increase at least 10% over the next five years.
Bargains Based on Earnings Prospects: This lists stocks with low price-earnings ratios relative to their projected five-year earnings growth rates.

Value Line Investment Survey
Value Line Publishing Inc., 220 E. 42nd St., New York, N.Y. 10017-5891, 800/634-3583. valueline.com.
Part 1 Summary & Index:
The tables in the back (see index for the page numbers) include these useful lists:
Widest Discounts from Book Value: This consists of stocks whose ratios of recent price to book value are the lowest.
Lowest P/Es: This consists of stocks whose current price-earnings ratios based on estimated earnings are the lowest.
Bargain Basement Stocks: These firms have low price-earnings ratios as well as price-to-net-working-capital (current assets less all liabilities) ratios that are in the bottom quartile of Value Line stocks.

Standard & Poor's Industry Reports
This is a monthly review of 115 industries and some 1,100 stocks. In the back of the industry reports are one-line listings for the selected companies within each industry, allowing for comparison of the various firms listed relative to others in the same industry. For each stock, the S&P's earnings and dividend rank, and S&P's evaluation of its investment potential (using their Stock Appreciation Ranking System) is included, which allows easy selection and comparison.

THE INITIAL LIST

Suggested sources from which you can draw your initial list of potential undervalued stocks are presented in the table on the opposing page. Many may be available in your local library. For computer users, an initial list of candidates can be compiled by applying various screens to a database of stocks. Appendix E (on page 73) discusses screens that are useful for the low price-earnings ratio approach.

The initial lists suggested here for beginners include not only lists of stocks with low price-earnings ratios, but also lists of stocks with other indications of undervaluation, such as low price-to-book value. Certain industries will dominate any list of stocks ranked only by price-earnings ratio. In addition, focusing only on stocks with the lowest ratios may turn up a list of stocks with no growth potential. Using other qualifying screens and indications of undervaluation will expand your universe of potential value plays and will help ensure that you do not accidentally concentrate too much on one specific industry.

Cyclical firms are likely to appear on many lists, so it would be useful to examine earnings growth over time periods covering at least one economic cycle to make sure you are focusing on long-term earnings trends. In addition, firms with years of negative earnings are likely to turn up. Negative earnings per share produce meaningless price-earnings ratios, and it can be difficult to form a judgment concerning a stock's average price-earnings ratio if there are several years with meaningless numbers. Examining a firm's price-earnings ratio over a much longer time period—perhaps even 10 years—may help. The tradeoff, however, is that the company may have changed fundamentally over this time.

Lastly, keep in mind that this is a contrarian strategy. The written analyses about the firms or industries that appear in these lists may not be particularly enthusiastic and many may be quite negative. It is important to understand why most analysts hold the views they do, and most often they are correct. It may take some digging combined with independent judgment on your part to find potentially undervalued firms.

Once a potential stock is spotted, the next step is an in-depth evaluation to determine the fair market value.

CHRYSLER CORP.: AN EXAMPLE

Chrysler Corp. offers a good example of the low price-earnings ratio approach to valuation. In July of 1994, Chrysler appeared in the Value Line list of stocks with the lowest price-earnings ratios; Ford and GM also appeared on the list, although Chrysler was the lowest. It had a low earnings and dividend ranking (B–) from Standard & Poor's, but was rated in the highest category for appreciation potential by Standard & Poor's (reported in S&P's Industry Reports).

Chrysler is the third largest automobile and truck manufacturer in the U.S. It is in a cyclical industry that was hurt badly by the 1990-1991 recession but then staged a strong turnaround during 1993. According to Value Line, the firm in early 1994 had strong sales, and in fact was at peak capacity for most of its vehicles.

Entering the per share data from an information source is relatively straightforward, but it is important to stick to the same source for company information, since reporting services make different adjustments to the data they provide. Value Line is used for the data here and the earnings figures include non-recurring gains and losses.

A Tour Through the Worksheet: Per Share Information

The first item of note is the price—on this date, June 30, 1994, it was between its 1993 high and low; during 1993 the stock was at its five-year high.

The year-by-year earnings per share figures indicate how badly the firm fared during the early 1990s. Clearly earnings were increasing by 1994, but the five-year growth rate figure of 49% is unsustainable over the long term; earnings have increased, but are unlikely to continue at the same pace. Value Line projects earnings in 1994 to be up substantially, at $8.00 per share, an 18% increase over 1993.

Dividends were halved in 1991, but were increased slightly in 1993 and again in 1994. With the recovery in earnings, it was unlikely that dividends would drop further; using the five-year average dividend growth rate figure of –14% to project next year's dividends is misleading. The 1994 annual indicated dividend was $1.00.

Looking at the Financial Ratios

Earnings concerns appear to be driving the price of Chrysler stock.

The price-earnings ratio of Chrysler appears at a considerable low, relative to its five-year historical norms. However, most of these price-earnings levels were produced at a time of extremely poor earnings for Chrysler. In 1990, for instance, Chrysler had earnings per share of only $0.30. The extraordinarily high price-earnings multiple in 1990 of 68.0 is due in large part to this extraordinarily low earnings per share level and not due to high expectations for growth. Its end of June 1994 price-earnings ratio of 6.2, however, was slightly below its average for 1993.

Chrysler's dividend yield paints a somewhat different picture. It had dropped substantially from its 1990 high of 9.5%. High dividend yields can indicate a good value (high dividends at a low price), or they may indicate that the market feels the dividend is in jeopardy—a feeling that was justified by the dividend cut in 1991. Dividend yields are most useful as indicators of value when dividends have held steady, and in Chrysler's case they had not. The "current" dividend yield of 2.1% was still below the level reached after the dividend cut, but above its 1993 high.

The payout ratio (dividends per share divided by earnings per share) helps gauge the strength of the dividend: The lower the payout ratio, the better, implying that the dividend payment is more secure. A 100% payout ratio shows that a firm is paying out all of its earnings to its shareholders. The payout ratio for Chrysler ranged all over the board, but indicated that the dividend was not in jeopardy.

The 1993 return on equity for Chrysler Corp. was above the industry average. Again, however, the historical figures are difficult to interpret. The return on equity measures how well the firm is being run on both an operational and financial basis. To boost

Valuation Worksheet

Company: Chrysler   **Current Price $** 47.50   **Date (** 6 / 30 / 94 **)**

Ticker C   **Exchange** NYSE   **Current P/E** 6.2   **Current Yield** 2.1%

Financial Statement & Ratio Analysis

Per Share Information	\multicolumn{6}{Company}						Industry or Competitor		Market
	19 89	19 90	19 91	19 92	19 93	5-year avg	19 93	5-year avg	19 93
Price: High	29.60	20.40	15.90	33.90	58.40				
Price: Low	18.10	9.10	9.80	11.50	31.80				
Earnings per Share (EPS)	1.36	0.30	–2.74	1.38	6.77	growth rate: 49%			
Dividends per Share (DPS)	1.20	1.20	0.60	0.60	0.65	growth rate: –14%			
Book Value per Share (BV)	32.42	30.53	20.91	25.47	19.32				
Financial Ratios									
Price-Earnings Ratio (P/E): Avg	17.5	49.2	NMF	16.4	6.7	22.5*	11.5	NMF	21.3
High (High Price ÷ EPS)	21.8	68.0	NMF	24.6	8.6	30.7*			
Low (Low Price ÷ EPS)	13.3	30.3	NMF	8.3	4.7	14.2*			
Dividend Yield % (DY): Avg	5.3	9.5	4.9	3.5	1.5	4.9	2.2	4.5**	2.7
High (DPS ÷ Low Price)	6.6	13.2	6.1	5.2	2.0	6.6			
Low (DPS ÷ High Price)	4.1	5.9	3.8	1.8	1.1	3.3			
Payout Ratio % (DPS ÷ EPS)	88.2	400	–21.9	43.5	9.6	135.2*	33.0	NMF	
Return on Equity % (EPS ÷ BV)	4.2	1.0	NMF	5.4	35.0	11.4*	25.4	NMF	
Financial Leverage %	235	186	245	178	100	189	327	259**	

*An average of 4 years, which excludes 1991.   ** 1990 through 1993.   NMF: no meaningful figure

Valuation Estimates

Model based on earnings:

Average high P/E × estimated 19 94 EPS: 30.7   × $8.00   = $245.60   (high valuation estimate)

Average low P/E × estimated 19 94 EPS: 14.2   × $8.00   = $113.60   (low valuation estimate)

Model based on dividends:

Estimated 19 94 annual DPS ÷ average low DY: $1.00   ÷ 0.033   = $30.30   (high valuation estimate)

Estimated 19 94 annual DPS ÷ average high DY: $1.00   ÷ 0.066   = $15.15   (low valuation estimate)

Use decimal form for DY. For instance 5.4% would be 0.054.

return on equity, a company must increase the profit margin on goods being sold, make better use of its assets, or increase the level of financial leverage. Chrysler's use of financial leverage, however, had been decreasing—and was below the industry norm. When times were good, Chrysler was reducing its debt.

VALUING THE COMPANY

The bottom of the Valuation Worksheet provides valuations using both the earnings-based model and dividend-based models.

The first item that needs to be determined is the appropriate per share earnings figure for 1994. The worksheet uses the more conservative Value Line estimate of $8.00 rather than a figure based on historical growth, since the five-year earnings growth rate is misleading.

Another problem is the average price-earnings ratio figure. The figure used on the worksheet uses four years (1991 is excluded because the negative earnings per share figure for that year produces meaningless figures). This produces a high valuation estimate of $245.60 and a low valuation estimate of $113.60. The price-earnings ratio in 1990 of 49.2, however, was extraordinarily high, due to the extremely low earnings per share figure that year. Excluding this year from the estimates, and using price-earnings ratios from only three years, would produce a high valuation of $146.40 and a low valuation of $70.40.

An even better approach, however, would be to examine the price-earnings ratio over a much longer time period—for instance, 10 years. This time period covers a complete economic cycle, and would provide a more appropriate price-earnings range. Using these figures (but still excluding 1990) provides a high valuation of $79.76 and a low valuation of $40.47.

Chrysler's June 1994 price of $47.50 was in the low range even using the 10-year averages, but it was not the obvious buy that it appeared at first blush using the five-year figures.

The 1994 indicated dividend of $1.00 per share is used in the dividend valuation model. The dividend model produces a high valuation of $30.30 and a low valuation of $15.15, based on the five-year high and low dividend yield averages. Ten-year dividend yield averages would produce a high valuation of $33.89 and a low valuation of $18.16. Chrysler clearly appeared overvalued based on the dividend yield model.

Which model is more appropriate? The stock at that time was priced considerably above the valuations based on the dividend yield model. It is far more likely that earnings expectations, rather than dividend considerations, are supporting the price of the stock.

The earnings models produced a wide range of valuations. Which one is most useful? Valuations based on earnings can be problematic for cyclical stocks, particularly if they are at their high points. The valuations based on the 10-year historical ratios are probably the most appropriate but still pose difficulties for a cyclical company. A more conservative approach would be to use the 10-year average *low* price-earnings ratio as the norm, and to purchase the stock only if it falls below the valuation based on that ratio. Using an average of its earnings per share over the last five years instead of 1994 estimated earnings per share would also be more conservative. Using either of these as a guide, Chrysler at that time would appear to be overvalued, or at least fairly valued.

CONCLUSION

While the worksheet examines quantitative factors, it is clear that many subjective factors go into the equation. Any final decision should be based on a better understanding of the company, its management, and its competitive environment.

Appendix E

Using Low P/E Screens to Find Undervalued Stocks

The price-earnings ratio is one of the most basic measures of value for investors. The price-earnings ratio, or multiple, is computed by dividing a stock's price by its most recent 12 months' earnings per share. The price-earnings ratio is followed so closely because it embodies the market's expectations of future company performance through the price component of the ratio and relates it to historical company performance as measured by earnings per share. This appendix will explore some of the basic price-earnings ratio techniques employed in screening a database for undervalued stocks.

Many studies point to profitability of investing in out-of-favor stocks. Value investors seek out firms with low price-earnings ratios with the belief that the market may have overreacted to negative news and is not correctly discounting their future earnings potential. A simple search for low price-earnings ratios, however, can be misleading as a guide to undervalued stocks. Typically, firms with high growth potential trade with correspondingly high price-earnings ratios while those with low price-earnings ratios are expected to have low growth. Screening just for stocks with a low price-earnings ratio may leave you with a list of companies with little or no growth prospects.

The results of the screening on the following pages illustrate the problems associated in screening for low price-earnings stocks. AAII's *Stock Investor* database of 8,000 stocks was used to perform the screening. The first screening filter excluded financial firms because their non-standard financial statements do not allow for direct comparison with firms in other industries. The next set of filters required that the firms have five years of data and that earnings per share be positive for the last 12 months. The tables present the 20 securities with the lowest price-earnings ratio that passed the screens. The price-earnings ratios for the these securities ranged from 1.3 to 4.2 compared to the S&P 500's price-earnings ratio at that time of 19.2. The screening used data that was current as of June 30, 1994.

Any screen requires detailed analysis to be performed on the resulting list of companies, and for good reason. This list is loaded with troubled firms. Studies indicating the advantages of investing in low price-earnings stocks use large portfolios of stocks to reduce the higher risk of investing in any single stock. Littlefield, Adams, for example, at the time of the screen was burdened by the uncertainty of an SEC investigation examining a wide range of corporate activities. Raytech Corp. had been operating under Chapter 11 bankruptcy protection since 1989 and had a cloud of over 3,000 asbestos-related lawsuits hanging over its head. Also, some of the securities that passed the screen are not corporations. For example, Samson Energy is a master limited partnership involved in the production, development, and acquisition of oil and gas drilling operations, a relatively high-risk and uncertain activity that often leads to lower price multiples.

In looking at the tables you may notice that only a few of the securities have information entered for the average and relative price-earnings valuation models. A weakness of using the price-earnings ratio for analysis is that dividing price by a negative earnings per share figure produces a meaningless number.

USING HISTORICAL AVERAGES

One useful way to use price-earnings ratios is to compare current multiples against historical averages. A current price-earnings ratio lower than its historical average would be a potential sign that a stock is undervalued, while a current price-earnings ratio that is high compared to its historical average might indicate an overvalued firm. Models that examine historical averages assume that the growth prospects of the firm have not changed fundamentally over time and, based on historical relationships of price to earnings, the market is not correctly discounting the future earnings potential of the firm.

To help illustrate the valuation aspect of the average price-earnings model, it is common to multiply the five-year average price-earnings ratio by the most recent 12 months' earnings per share to arrive at a price estimate. Comparing this valuation price to the stock's current price provides a useful ratio for screening stocks. Table 2 provides the results of a stock screen based upon the average price-earnings ratio. The information pertaining to the average price-earnings model is highlighted.

Because the screen relies on the five-year average price-earnings ratio, this screening required that the firms have five years of positive earnings per share. This is why so many of the firms listed in Table 1 did not make it into Table 2. Beyond negative earnings, which lead to meaningless price-earnings ratios, unusually low earnings may also throw off standard price-earnings ratio screens. Short-term drops in earnings due to events such as special charges, extraordinary events, or in some cases even recessions may lead to unusually high price-earnings ratios. As long as the market interprets the earnings decrease as temporary, the high price-earnings ratio will be supported. Because the average price-earnings model relies on a normal situation, these "outlier" price-earnings ratios must be excluded. When performing a hands-on evaluation you can manually exclude years with negative earnings or unusually high price-earnings ratios. However, when screening a large universe of stocks, it is best to establish criteria that eliminate companies with extreme price-earnings ratios. For the average price-earnings screen, companies with ratios above 100 for any of the last five fiscal years were excluded. If you want to be more conservative, a tighter requirement, such as ratios above 40 or 50, might be specified.

Definitions of Screens and Terms

EPS Last 12 Mo.: Earnings from continuing operations for the most recent 12 months divided by the number of common shares outstanding.

P/E Ratio: Market price per share divided by most recent 12 months' earnings per share. A measure of the market's expectations regarding the firm's earnings growth and risk.

5-Year Average P/E Ratio: An average of the high and low price-earnings ratios for the past five years. Provides a base level to compare the current price-earnings ratio.

Average P/E Share Valuation: Five-year average price-earnings ratio multiplied by earnings per share for the most recent 12 months. Gives an estimate of price supported by historical price-earnings average. Can also be computed with expected future earnings per share.

Ratio of Avg. P/E Valuation to Current Price: Estimated average price-earnings share valuation divided by current price. A ratio of 1.00 indicates that the valuation estimate is equal to the current price. A ratio above 1.00 indicates an undervalued security while a ratio below 1.00 indicates an overvalued security.

5-Year P/E Relative: Ratio of historical company price-earnings levels relative to those of the S&P 500 index. Provides an indication as to whether the company traditionally trades at a premium or discount to the market.

P/E Relative Share Valuation: Price-earnings relative multiplied by the company earnings per share. Gives an estimate of stock price value supported by the historical relationship of the price-earnings ratio to the market's, and the current market and company situation. Can also be computed with expected company earnings per share.

Ratio of P/E Rel. Valuation to Current Price: Estimated price-earnings relative share valuation divided by current price. A ratio of 1.00 indicates that the valuation estimate is equal to the current price. A ratio above 1.00 indicates an undervalued security; a ratio below 1.00 indicates an overvalued security.

The top 20 firms ranked on the ratio of average price-earnings valuation to current price are shown in Table 2. To arrive at the valuation, the earnings per share for the last 12 months was multiplied by average price-earnings ratio.

Table 4 illustrates the calculations involved in the average price-earnings model. The Boston Celtics Limited Partnership owns and operates the Boston Celtics as well as a Boston radio and television station. Five years prior to June 1994, the price-earnings ratio of Boston Celtics had trended up as the price largely stayed flat and earnings had decreased. The average price-earnings ratio over those five years was 14.8. Multiplying the earnings per share for the last 12 months by the average price-earnings ratio leads to a valuation of $41.59. This is 2.08 times the June 30, 1994 price. Boston Celtics just missed making the listing in Table 2, but made the listing in Table 3, which is based upon the price-earnings relative model.

One weakness with average price-earnings approach is that it looks purely at historical relationships, while the current market price is driven by future expectations. The

Table 1. Low Price-Earnings Ratio Screen
Ranked by Price-Earnings Ratio

company (exchange)	price as of 6/30/94 ($)	EPS last 12 mos ($)	P/E ratio (x)	5-yr avg P/E ratio (x)	avg P/E share val'n ($)	ratio of avg P/E val'n to price (x)	5-yr P/E rel (x)	P/E rel share val'n ($)	ratio of P/E rel val'n to price (x)	description
Littlefield, Adams (AM)	4.81	3.58	1.3	nmf	nmf	nmf	nmf	nmf	nmf	Engages in the imprinting of athletic wear
Advanced Semicon (NM)	2.63	1.60	1.6	nmf	nmf	nmf	nmf	nmf	nmf	Mfrs equip to produce semiconductor devices
Samson Energy LP (AM)	8.63	5.26	1.6	nmf	nmf	nmf	nmf	nmf	nmf	Prod, devlp, acquisition of oil & gas prop
Raytech Corp. (NY)	4.50	2.67	1.7	4.5	12.02	2.67	0.22	11.51	2.56	Mfrs asbestos & other friction prods
Castle Energy (NM)	14.50	8.00	1.8	nmf	nmf	nmf	nmf	nmf	nmf	Explor'n, devlp, produc'n oil & gas
Norex America (AM)	9.00	5.11	1.8	nmf	nmf	nmf	nmf	nmf	nmf	Mkts, provides leisure cruises
America West Airlines (NM)	3.75	1.88	2.0	nmf	nmf	nmf	nmf	nmf	nmf	Regional airline service
Audiovox Corp. (AM)	6.88	3.47	2.0	nmf	nmf	nmf	nmf	nmf	nmf	Mkts, distribs automotive aftermarket prods
WPP Group PLC (NM)	2.94	1.45	2.0	10.5	15.23	5.18	0.57	16.20	5.51	Multi-national marketing services
LVI Group Inc. (NY)	0.63	0.29	2.2	nmf	nmf	nmf	nmf	nmf	nmf	Electrical equipment distributors
Fairchild Corp. A (NY)	3.88	1.58	2.5	nmf	nmf	nmf	nmf	nmf	nmf	Motor freight carrier & aircraft replacem't parts
Buffton Corp. (AM)	1.19	0.42	2.8	nmf	nmf	nmf	nmf	nmf	nmf	Mfrs avionic, electronic, plastic products
Highwood Restaurant (NM)	0.75	0.26	2.9	nmf	nmf	nmf	nmf	nmf	nmf	Explores strategic, rare-earths, precious metals
Hathaway Corp. (NM)	4.00	1.19	3.4	nmf	nmf	nmf	nmf	nmf	nmf	Mfrs, sells elec pwr record equip, elec motrs
Salant Corp. (NY)	7.00	1.89	3.7	nmf	nmf	nmf	nmf	nmf	nmf	Mfrs, mkts apparel prods for entire family
Allied Research Corp. (AM)	4.19	1.09	3.8	nmf	nmf	nmf	nmf	nmf	nmf	Devlps, prods weapons systems, ammo
Instrumentarium (NS)	11.25	2.89	3.9	nmf	nmf	nmf	nmf	nmf	nmf	Distribs hospital equip and supplies
IP Timberlands LP (NY)	24.13	6.02	4.0	6.1	36.72	1.52	0.35	41.30	1.71	Forest resource management
Maxco Inc. (NM)	8.25	2.06	4.0	12.1	24.93	3.02	0.75	30.28	3.67	Engineers, fabricates special welding machine
Flanigan Enterprises (AM)	4.00	0.96	4.2	nmf	nmf	nmf	nmf	nmf	nmf	Pkg liquor stores, cocktail liquor

nmf = no meaningful figure

Exchanges: NY = New York Stock Exchange; AM = American Stock Exchange; NM = Nasdaq National Market; NS = Nasdaq Small Cap

Sources: Stock Investor/Media General; I/B/E/S; and S&P Stock Guide. All data as of June 30, 1994.

Table 2. Price-Earnings Average Screen Ranked by the Ratio of Valuation Based on Average P/E to Current Price

company (exchange)	price as of 6/30/94 ($)	EPS last 12 mos ($)	P/E ratio (x)	5-yr avg P/E ratio (x)	avg P/E share val'n ($)	ratio of avg P/E val'n to price (x)	5-yr P/E rel (x)	P/E rel share val'n ($)	ratio of P/E rel val'n to price (x)	description
Georgia Bonded (NM)	5.00	1.04	4.8	32.5	33.80	6.76	1.88	38.32	7.66	Mfrs elastomeric impregnated paper prods
WPP Group PLC (NM)	2.94	1.45	2.0	10.5	15.23	5.18	0.57	16.20	5.51	Multi-national marketing services
Adac Laboratories (NM)	8.38	1.23	6.8	34.4	42.31	5.05	1.71	41.23	4.92	Nuclear medicine computer systems
LaBarge Inc. (AM)	1.19	0.16	7.4	35.8	5.73	4.82	2.18	6.84	5.75	Mfrs tubular, modular, electrical prods
Merisel Inc. (NM)	8.75	1.07	8.2	37.0	39.59	4.52	2.15	45.09	5.15	Wholesale microcomp'r hardware & software
Holly Corp. (AM)	28.50	3.87	7.4	25.8	99.85	3.50	1.35	102.40	3.59	Refining, explor'g, produc'g petroleum
Research Indus (NM)	8.00	0.60	13.3	44.4	26.64	3.33	2.41	28.34	3.54	Sales health care prods & real estate development
Dresser Indus (NY)	20.50	2.17	9.4	31.3	67.92	3.31	1.68	71.46	3.49	Supplier of prods & serv to oil & gas cos
ACC Corp. (NM)	13.75	1.70	8.1	26.7	45.39	3.30	1.37	45.65	3.32	Diversified telecomm'ns company
Teltronics Inc. (NS)	9.00	0.75	12.0	36.5	27.38	3.04	1.92	28.22	3.14	Mfrs telecommun equip
Anacomp Inc. (NY)	3.00	0.22	13.6	38.1	8.38	2.79	2.38	10.26	3.42	Provides computer & micrograph serv
Times Mirror (NY)	30.13	2.41	12.5	34.5	83.15	2.76	1.83	86.45	2.87	News & book publish, info serv, TV
USA Waste Service (NY)	11.63	0.79	14.7	39.8	31.44	2.70	2.34	36.23	3.12	Provides solid waste management and serv
Raytech Corp. (NY)	4.50	2.67	1.7	4.5	12.02	2.67	0.22	11.51	2.56	Mfrs asbestos & other friction prods
Dorchester Hugoton (NM)	13.25	0.94	14.1	36.8	34.59	2.61	2.04	37.58	2.84	Partnership in oil & gas properties
Providence & Worch'r (NM)	7.50	0.54	13.9	35.6	19.22	2.56	2.15	22.76	3.03	Operates interstate freight system
General Microwave (AM)	7.88	0.76	10.4	26.4	20.06	2.55	1.43	21.30	2.70	Electronic measurement and control equip
Pennzoil Co. (NY)	51.25	3.38	15.2	37.8	127.76	2.49	2.10	139.12	2.71	Explor, produc oil & gas; mfrs refined petro prods
Pacific Telecom (NM)	21.75	3.06	7.1	17.7	54.16	2.49	0.96	57.59	2.65	Telephone communic'n serv
Surgical Care (NY)	13.25	0.95	13.9	34.2	32.49	2.45	1.80	33.52	2.53	Devlps, owns outpatient surgical care facilities

nmf = no meaningful figure

Exchanges: NY = New York Stock Exchange; AM = American Stock Exchange; NM = Nasdaq National Market; NS = Nasdaq Small Cap

Sources: Stock Investor/Media General; I/B/E/S; and S&P Stock Guide. All data as of June 30, 1994.

Table 3. Price-Earnings Relative Screen Ranked by the Ratio of Valuation Based on P/E Relative to Current Price

company (exchange)	price as of 6/30/94 ($)	EPS last 12 mos ($)	P/E ratio (x)	5-yr avg P/E ratio (x)	avg P/E share val'n ($)	ratio of avg P/E val'n to price (x)	5-yr P/E rel (x)	P/E rel share val'n ($)	ratio of P/E rel val'n to price (x)	description
WPP Group PLC (NM)	2.94	1.45	2.0	10.5	15.23	5.18	0.57	16.20	5.51	Multi-national marketing services
Seneca Foods (NM)	22.50	3.01	7.5	18.0	54.18	2.41	1.00	59.00	2.62	Food processing; distrib services
Raytech Corp. (NY)	4.50	2.67	1.7	4.5	12.02	2.67	0.22	11.51	2.56	Mfrs asbestos & other friction prods
Merrimac Indus (AM)	8.38	1.16	7.2	15.5	17.98	2.15	0.86	19.56	2.33	Component/subsystem in signal process
Bowne & Co. (AM)	20.75	2.39	8.7	17.0	40.63	1.96	1.01	47.32	2.28	Finance & corporation printing
Lynch Corp. (AM)	26.38	3.56	7.4	14.9	53.04	2.01	0.85	59.31	2.25	Diversified manuf'g activities
Boston Celtics (NY)	20.00	2.81	7.1	14.8	41.59	2.08	0.81	44.62	2.23	Professional basketball team
Napco Security Sys (NM)	3.13	0.47	6.7	13.7	6.44	2.06	0.74	6.82	2.18	Mfrs security alarm prods
Park Electrochemical (NY)	28.75	2.58	11.1	22.0	56.76	1.97	1.23	62.20	2.16	Prints circuit materials
Robinson Nugent (NM)	5.75	0.47	12.2	24.3	11.42	1.99	1.33	12.25	2.13	Sockets & custom electromechan'l prods
Sun Microsystems (NM)	20.63	1.94	10.6	19.9	38.61	1.87	1.12	42.58	2.06	Supplies network-based computing systems
PSICOR Inc. (NM)	9.25	1.01	9.2	17.1	17.27	1.87	0.96	19.01	2.06	Provides perfusionist equip to hospitals
B.A.T. Indus PLC (AM)	12.31	1.19	10.3	19.3	22.97	1.87	1.07	24.95	2.03	Mfrs tobacco prods
REFAC Tech Devlp (AM)	7.00	0.79	8.9	15.5	12.25	1.75	0.91	14.09	2.01	Admins interna'l technology licenses
Plasti-Line (NM)	7.50	0.72	10.4	19.0	13.68	1.82	1.06	14.96	1.99	Designs, mkts illuminated outdoor signs
GTI Corp. (NM)	10.25	1.15	8.9	16.9	19.44	1.90	0.90	20.29	1.98	Mfrs electronic sealer components
Top Air Mfg (NS)	0.88	0.07	12.6	24.9	1.74	1.98	1.26	1.73	1.97	Designs, mfrs, sells agricultural equip
Bridgford Foods (NM)	8.31	0.62	13.4	25.0	15.50	1.87	1.33	16.16	1.94	Makes, distributes frozen foods
Utah Medical Prods (NM)	6.88	0.60	11.5	20.6	12.36	1.80	1.11	13.06	1.90	Dev/mfrs/mkts medical devices
United Stationers (NM)	9.75	1.15	8.5	15.0	17.25	1.77	0.82	18.48	1.90	Distribs wholesale office prods

nmf = no meaningful figure
Exchanges: NY = New York Stock Exchange; AM = American Stock Exchange; NM = Nasdaq National Market; NS = Nasdaq Small Cap

Sources: Stock Investor/Media General; I/B/E/S; and S&P Stock Guide. All data as of June 30, 1994.

Table 4.
Sample Calculations Using
Boston Celtics LP as an Example

	S&P 500					Boston Celtics							
	index value		EPS	P/E ratio		stock price		EPS	P/E ratio		P/E relative to market	
	high ($)	low ($)	($)	high (×)	low (×)	high ($)	low ($)	($)	high (×)	low (×)	high (×)	low (×)
1989	$359.80	$275.31	$22.87	15.7	12.0	$19.500	$13.500	$1.88	10.4	7.2	0.66	0.60
1990	$368.95	$295.46	$21.34	17.3	13.9	$19.125	$14.500	$1.23	15.6	11.8	0.90	0.85
1991	$417.09	$311.49	$15.97	26.1	19.5	$20.875	$16.125	$1.69	12.4	9.5	0.47	0.49
1992	$441.28	$394.50	$21.95	20.1	18.0	$23.875	$16.250	$1.19	20.1	13.7	1.00	0.76
1993	$470.94	$429.05	$21.88	21.5	19.6	$21.625	$16.375	$0.80	27.0	20.5	1.26	1.04
5-year average				20.1	16.6				17.1	12.5	0.86	0.75
5-year average (combined high & low)				18.4					14.8		0.81	

As of June 30, 1994:

S&P Price-Earnings Ratio	19.6
Stock Price	$20.00
Earnings per Share (last 12 mos.)	$2.81
Price-Earnings Ratio	7.1

Average P/E Model

Share Valuation

= Average P/E Ratio × EPS
= 14.8 × $2.81
= $41.59

Ratio of Share Valuation to Current Price

= Valuation ÷ Current Price
= $41.59 ÷ $20.00
= 2.08

P/E Relative Model

Adjusted P/E

= Current Market P/E × Average P/E Relative
= 19.6 × 0.81
= 15.9

Share Valuation

= Adjusted P/E × EPS
= 15.9 × $2.81
= $44.68

Ratio of Share Valuation to Current Price

= Valuation ÷ Current Price
= $44.68 ÷ $20.00
= 2.23

trailing 12-month earnings per share figure may be unusually high or low due to a one-time event, or the historical average may not reflect a change in the company, industry, or economic environment. For the Boston Celtics Limited Partnership, the trailing earnings per share figure of $2.81 represents a tremendous increase over the $0.80 for the last fiscal year. Much of this earnings increase can be attributed to the selling of an option to Fox Television providing the right to purchase a 26% ownership interest in the television station owned by the partnership. The earnings figure also includes an insurance settlement involving the death of a Celtics basketball player.

To get around the limitation of historical earnings per share, estimated earnings can be used. Consensus earnings estimates, however, are usually only available for larger, more actively followed companies. A screen requiring consensus earnings estimates will exclude a number of interesting neglected stocks.

PRICE-EARNINGS RELATIVE MODELS

Another way to use price-earnings ratios is to compare them with the industry price-earnings ratio, or even the overall market ratio. Based upon economic conditions and factors, the fair value of the market can change. For example, the market can support higher price-earnings ratios under the condition of low interest rates than it can under high interest rate conditions. The price-earnings relative is determined by dividing a company's price-earnings ratio by that of the market. Based on relative growth and risk expectations, companies trade at market multiples greater or smaller than that of the market. One would expect a company with prospects better than the market or with lower risk to have a higher price-earnings ratio than the market. Comparing a firm to its industry is an equally useful technique that has the benefit of isolating interesting candidates within a specific industry.

A price-earnings relative above 1.00 would indicate that a company's price-earnings ratio is typically above the market's price-earnings ratio, while a price-earnings relative below 1.00 would indicate that a company's price-earnings ratios tends to be lower than the market's. By averaging the price-earnings relative over time, you can estimate a price-earnings relative that a stock tends to follow.

Table 4 also illustrates the calculations used to determine the price-earnings relative. Over the five years prior to the screen, the Boston Celtics averaged a price-earnings multiple below that of the S&P 500 leading to an average price-earnings relative of 0.81. Multiplying the price-earnings relative by the market's current price-earnings ratio provides an adjusted stock price-earnings ratio. The assumption is that the market is fairly valued and that the company's relationship to the market has not changed. A stock price valuation can be determined by multiplying this adjusted stock price-earnings ratio by the earnings per share figure. The ratio of the valuation to the current price provides a useful screening measure. Table 3 is based upon this ratio of valuation determined by the price-earnings relative valuation divided by the current price.

To eliminate outliers, the high limit for the price-earnings ratio was tied to the market's price-earnings level. Companies whose price-earnings ratios were more than double the market's in any year were excluded. This filter was more stringent than the one used with the average price-earnings ratio screen, creating a more conservative screen and leading to a largely different list of companies in Table 3 than in Table 2.

The companies passing these screens were sorted based upon their ratio of price-earnings relative share valuation to current price, with the top 20 firms listed in Table 3. The fields pertaining to the price-earnings relative model are highlighted. As with the previous screens, the list is made up of companies that had fallen out of favor, such as B.A.T. Industries and Sun Microsystems. B.A.T. is a tobacco company that in mid-1994 was caught in the midst of a storm surrounding the tobacco industry. Sun Microsystems, once a high-flying computer workstation manufacturer, had seen its earnings decline in recent years. Both firms find their July 1994 price-earnings ratios hovering at about half the market level of 19.6, not at their historical slight premium to the market.

CONCLUSION

Screening for stocks by looking at price-earnings ratios can help highlight firms that have fallen out of favor. As in any technique, there are many ways to take a simple rule and expand upon it to meet your objectives. Looking at just low price-earnings stocks will highlight companies the market is neglecting, but this screen also tends to highlight the most troubled issues that require very detailed analysis. It is also common for low price-earnings screens to be dominated by a few industries that are currently out of favor.

Screening based upon an examination of the average price-earnings ratio allows you to seek out companies that have fallen out of favor, but may not be as troubled as firms from the pure low price-earnings screen. The average price-earnings model looks to past earnings valuation to help set a benchmark comparison. It identifies firms that have deviated from their normal valuation level, with the expectation that they will move back toward their typical levels. This model also has its weaknesses: It assumes that nothing fundamental to the company, industry, or market has significantly changed.

The primary benefit of the price-earnings relative model over the average price-earnings ratio is that it allows for adjustments to broad economic changes affecting the market. It identifies those stocks that have deviated from their long-term relationships to a benchmark index, while still assuming a stable company relationship to the market over time. As with all of the techniques presented, industries that have fallen out of favor may dominate the analysis.

This chapter has focused purely on identifying primary screening criteria. Screening for low price-earnings firms turns up companies that have fallen out of favor, some for good reasons. In constructing screening criteria, you may wish to include a number of conditioning criteria that help indicate items such as the future earnings potential of the firm, the financial strength of the firm, as well as the strength of the firm within its industry. Investing in low price-earnings stocks can be rewarding, but caution is required.

Using Analysts' Estimates To Your Advantage

When purchasing a stock, an investor must first form an expectation concerning the outlook for the company and the stock's price. But stock prices are driven by market expectations—the overall expectations of all investors—and stock prices change as the market's expectations change.

Tracking those expectations can provide some clues to the future direction of a stock's price. This can be done by examining the earnings estimates made by analysts at major investment research firms who follow the stock.

This chapter focuses on a basic approach that takes advantage of changes in expectations to turn up promising candidates. Appendix F (on page 89) discusses in detail the ways in which earnings estimates can be tracked using computer-based services, and how they can be used to screen a large database of stocks.

Stock Characteristics

Research on earnings estimates indicates that investing in stocks of companies with significant upward revisions in analysts' earnings estimates and positive earnings surprises leads to above-average returns. An earnings surprise occurs when a company announces earnings that are significantly different from analysts' consensus expectations.

If any general company characteristic can be associated with stocks that have earnings surprises, it is that they are in a state of change and uncertainty. The environment of uncertainty may come out of an overall economic change, such as an economy on the verge of a turnaround. Right now, for instance, screens for stocks with earnings surprises and positive revisions in analysts' earnings estimates are filled with cyclical companies that are experiencing stronger sales than expected. A change within an industry, such as the unanticipated impact of a new regulation or even a change within an individual company such as the use of new technology, may also cause uncertainty.

The Initial List

Suggested sources from which you can draw your initial list are presented. Many may

Drawing Up an Initial List: Sources of Information

Analyst Watch
Zacks Investment Research Inc.
155 N. Wacker Dr., Chicago, Ill. 60606
800/399-6659
www.zacks.com
Monthly. Reports earnings estimates from analysts for over 6,000 stocks. Includes a section near the front called Criteria Screens, which has a large number of listings based on earnings estimates, including largest positive earnings revisions covering various periods and best earnings surprises.

Institutional Brokers' Estimate System (I/B/E/S)
Monthly Summary Data Book
1 World Trade Center, 18th Floor
New York, N.Y. 10048
212/437-8200
www.ibes.com
Monthly. Reports earnings estimates from analysts for over 4,000 stocks. The Highlights section provides a number of useful lists, including the 40 largest estimate increases over the previous month and companies with the largest positive quarterly earnings surprises.

Standard & Poor's Earnings Guide
Standard & Poor's Corp.
65 Broadway, 8th Floor New York, N.Y. 10006
800/221-5277
www.stockinfo.standardpoor.com
Monthly. Includes summary (one-line) information and focuses on earnings and earnings growth estimates from analysts. The front includes this useful list:
Significant Estimate Changes: These are firms that have had significant changes in earnings estimates from analysts since the previous month.
Two other lists appear periodically that may also be useful:
Substantial Estimate and Price Increases from Year-End: These are firms whose earnings estimates have increased since December of the previous year by at least 20% and whose stock prices have gone up by at least 20%.
Tight Earnings Projections: These are firms in which analysts' high and low estimates don't differ more than 10%. Given the tight range of estimates, any earnings "surprises" would have a large impact on these stocks.

Value Line Investment Survey
Value Line Publishing Inc.
220 E. 42nd St., New York, N.Y. 10017-5891
800/634-3583
valueline.com
Part 1 Summary & Index: Value Line provides its own earnings estimates for companies it covers. It does not have a separate list of companies with earnings revisions. However, the Summary has one-line listings for all companies, and indicates earnings revisions with an arrow next to the estimate. The tables in the back (see index for the page numbers) also includes this list:
Stocks Moving Up In Rank: This consists of stocks of firms who have moved up in Value Line's Timeliness ranks, primarily those caused by new earnings reports where earnings were higher than expected.

Sources of Earnings Estimates
The sources listed above are all published sources for earnings estimates. The following list shows information services that provide earnings estimates for the computer user; the source of the estimates is noted.

CompuServe (I/B/E/S)
800/848-8199

Stock Investor (I/B/E/S)
800/428-2244

Dow Jones News/
Retrieval (Zacks)
800/522-3567

Telescan (Zacks)
800/324-8246

be available in your local library. For computer users, an initial list of candidates can be compiled from the databases listed at the bottom of the box.

Earnings estimates can be used in a variety of ways, which Appendix F explores more fully. For the purpose of spotting promising candidates, you would want to concentrate on those firms that would benefit from changes in expectations. That would mean looking for these characteristics:

- Stocks of firms with significant positive revisions in the earnings expectations of analysts.
- Stocks of firms whose recent earnings reports significantly exceeded earnings expectations (a positive earnings surprise).
- Stocks of firms with a tight range of earnings estimates, where a positive earnings surprise would have the largest impact, or stocks of firms with a wide range of earnings estimates where a positive earnings surprise would be most likely.

Make sure that the list you are using is recent. Also keep in mind that the stocks selected under this approach are likely to receive a fair amount of coverage, making the likelihood of uncovering "hidden potential" unlikely. Only if you disagree with the consensus and feel earnings will once again come in higher than expected will there be the potential for above-average returns.

Once a potential stock is spotted, the next step is an in-depth evaluation to determine the fair market value. The following example is based on published information that was available in August of 1994, when the approach was applied.

NACCO Industries: An Example

NACCO Industries offers a good example of this approach. It was chosen because it turned up in several lists: It appeared in S&P's Earnings Guide in its list of Significant 1994 Estimate Changes, and in the Value Line Summary where an upward earnings revision was indicated in the summary listings.

NACCO Industries is classified in the machinery (construction and mining) industry, a cyclical industry. However, it is actually a holding company with three subsidiaries: a forklift manufacturing group (Hyster-Yale); a small appliance manufacturer (Hamilton Beach/Proctor-Silex); and a coal mining firm (North American Coal Corp.).

The industry as a whole, according to Value Line, had posted earnings above those that were expected due to better than expected sales both domestically and abroad. In line with this, NACCO's forklift manufacturing subsidiary had a large second quarter sales increase. Lower manufacturing costs also helped its other subsidiary, Hamilton Beach, in the second quarter. According to Value Line, the biggest concern facing investors is how soon this cyclical industry boom would peak and begin to drop off.

Value Line was used as the source of both company and industry information on the completed valuation worksheet presented for NACCO.

Per Share Information

The first item of note is the August 1994 price, which was near its high for 1993. The price had stayed within a wide range since 1990 and had not since risen above the top of this range.

At the same time, year-by-year earnings per share showed a fairly sharp drop over the years, from $5.26 in 1989 to only $1.30 in 1993, leading to a five-year growth rate of –29.5%. However, NACCO is a cyclical firm, and earnings in mid-1994 were heading up, not down. For that reason, the five-year earnings growth rate is not particularly useful in projecting the next year's earnings. The Value Line earnings estimate for 1994 was $4.35, an increase of 234% over 1993 earnings.

Dividends remained fairly steady over the prior five years, with a five-year growth rate of only 3.3%. Value Line's estimate of $0.68 shows a continuation of that modest increase.

LOOKING AT THE FINANCIAL RATIOS

The price-earnings ratio of NACCO, at 21.8 in mid-August 1994, was close to its five-year average high, and below its lowest level in 1993. However, the 1993 price-earnings range of 32.3 to 44.8 was extremely high due in large part to the cyclically low earnings per share level and not due to high expectations for growth. The abnormally high 1993 figures tend to distort the five-year average; a four-year average, excluding 1993, produces an average price-earnings ratio of 13.5, with a four-year average high of 18.0 and a four-year average low of 9.0. The August 1994 price-earnings ratio was above these four-year averages, in line with expectations at that time regarding earnings growth.

NACCO's dividend yield of 1.2% in August of 1994 was close to its five-year low. Dividend yields (dividends per share divided by price) are most useful as indicators of value when dividends have been significant and steady, which they have been. Normally, a low dividend yield relative to the historical level indicates a relatively high market valuation for the firm, if dividend considerations are a driving force behind the stock price.

NACCO's payout ratio in 1993 almost doubled, due to its abnormally low earnings per share figure for that year. A firm's payout ratio (dividends per share divided by earnings per share) helps gauge the strength of the dividend by indicating how much of a firm's earnings are paid out to shareholders. The lower the payout ratio, the better, implying dividend payments are more secure. Excluding 1993, NACCO's payout ratio had been low, indicating that the dividend was not in jeopardy. Earnings per share were expected to increase much more than dividends, so NACCO's payout ratio would likely drop back to pre-1993 levels.

The 1993 return on equity of 4.9% was below the industry average of 14.8%, although the abnormally low 1993 earnings per share figure distorts that year's return on equity figure. Return on equity measures how well the firm is managed both operationally and financially. To boost return on equity, a company must increase its profits from sales, manufacture its goods more efficiently, or increase the level of financial leverage. NACCO's use of financial leverage had been steadily decreasing, but it was above the

Valuation Worksheet

Company: NACCO Industries 'A'   **Current Price $** 58.00   **Date (** 8 / 12 / 94 **)**

Ticker NC   **Exchange** NYSE   **Current P/E** 21.8   **Current Yield** 1.2%

Financial Statement & Ratio Analysis

| Per Share Information | Company | | | | | 5-year avg | Industry or Competitor | | Market |
	19 89	19 90	19 91	19 92	19 93		19 93	5-year avg	19 93
Price: High	56.00	70.50	56.90	60.00	58.30				
Price: Low	31.30	22.00	29.00	34.30	42.00				
Earnings per Share (EPS)	5.26	4.87	2.31	2.71	1.30	growth rate: −29.5%			
Dividends per Share (DPS)	0.58	0.60	0.62	0.64	0.66	growth rate: 3.3%			
Book Value per Share (BV)	33.89	39.75	39.44	26.82	26.35				
Financial Ratios									
Price-Earnings Ratio (P/E): Avg	8.3	9.5	18.6	17.4	38.6	18.4	16.6	**	21.3
High (High Price ÷ EPS)	10.6	14.5	24.6	22.1	44.8	23.0			
Low (Low Price ÷ EPS)	6.0	4.5	12.6	12.7	32.3	13.9			
Dividend Yield % (DY): Avg	1.4	1.8	1.6	1.5	1.4	1.5	1.8	**	2.7
High (DPS ÷ Low Price)	1.9	2.7	2.1	1.9	1.6	2.0			
Low (DPS ÷ High Price)	1.0	0.9	1.1	1.1	1.1	1.0			
Payout Ratio % (DPS ÷ EPS)	11.0	12.3	26.8	23.6	50.8	24.4	30	**	
Return on Equity % (EPS ÷ BV)	15.5	12.3	5.9	10.1	4.9	10.7	14.8	6.2***	
Financial Leverage* %	240	234	213	192	152	206	80	68***	

*Long-term debt ÷ equity   **Not enough years with meaningful stats   ***1990 through 1993

Valuation Estimates

Model based on earnings:

Average high P/E × estimated 19 94 EPS: __23.0__ × __4.35__ = $100.05 (high) using 4-yr P/E: $78.30 (high)

Average low P/E × estimated 19 94 EPS: __13.9__ × __4.35__ = $60.46 (low) using 4-yr P/E: $39.15 (low)

Model based on dividends:

Estimated 19 94 annual DPS ÷ average low DY: __0.68__ ÷ __0.01__ = $68.00 (high valuation estimate)

Estimated 19 94 annual DPS ÷ average high DY: __0.68__ ÷ __0.02__ = $34.00 (low valuation estimate)

Use decimal form for DY. For instance 5.4% would be 0.054.

industry norm. One would expect to see a return on equity higher than the industry average with above-average financial leverage.

Valuing the Company

The bottom of the Valuation Worksheet provides valuations using both the earnings-based model and dividend-based models.

For the earnings-based models, the 1994 earnings per share figure used is the Value Line projection, since a projection based on the five-year average growth rate would be misleading. For the dividend-based models, the dividends per share figure is based on the five-year average growth rate, which matches the Value Line projection.

The five-year averages for the high and low price-earnings ratios and high and low dividend yields were also used in the worksheet. The results: The earnings-based models produced a valuation range of $60.46 to $100.05, while the dividend-based models produced a range of $34.00 to $68.00.

The valuations produced by the earnings model would indicate that the stock, in August 1994, was underpriced at a time when earnings expectations were clearly rising—an unlikely occurrence. That is reason to question the model's assumptions.

As we noted earlier, the five-year average price-earnings ratio figures are distorted by the abnormally high ratios in 1993. A four-year average that excludes 1993 would be more appropriate. Using the four-year average in the earnings-based model produces a valuation range of $39.15 to $78.30.

What about the dividend-based model? Since dividend considerations do not appear to be much of a factor affecting NACCO's price, this model is not useful here.

NACCO's price in August of 1994 was about $58.00, close to midpoint between the four-year high and four-year low earnings-based valuations. That indicates a fairly priced stock.

If you agree with the consensus outlook for earnings, as indicated by the Value Line estimates, don't expect to be rewarded by above-average returns. However, if you expect that earnings per share will come in higher than expected by the consensus, there will be a potential for another earnings surprise—and the potential for above-average returns.

Conclusion

A careful examination of the assumptions is a critical part of the valuation and will help you identify factors that could be misleading.

While the worksheet examines quantitative factors, it is clear that many subjective factors go into the equation. Any final decision should be based on a better understanding of the company, its management, and its competitive environment. This can only be accomplished by a thorough reading of the firm's financial reports, as well as the reports and summaries on the firm and its industry.

Appendix F

Analyzing Earnings Revisions

Investors quickly learn that the market is forward-looking. Security prices are established through expectations, and prices change as these expectations change or are proven incorrect. In the last 10 years, we have seen a significant increase in the services that track and analyze expected earnings per share estimates.

Services such as I/B/E/S, Nelson's, Standard & Poor's, and Zacks provide consensus earnings estimates by tracking the estimates of thousands of investment analysts. Tracking these expectations and their changes is an important and rewarding strategy for screening a database of stocks.

In using earnings estimates, the first rule to keep in mind is that the current price usually reflects the consensus earnings estimate. It is common to see price declines for stocks that report earnings increases from the previous reporting period because in many cases, while the actual earnings represent an increase, the increase is not as great as the market had expected. Earnings surprises occur when a company reports actual earnings that differ from consensus earnings estimates.

During the earnings reporting season, financial newspapers such as The Wall Street Journal provide daily reports on earnings announcements. Firms with significant earnings surprises are often highlighted.

Positive earnings surprises occur when actual reported earnings are significantly above the forecasted earnings per share. Negative earnings surprises occur when reported earnings per share are significantly below the earnings expectations. The stock prices of firms with significant positive earnings surprises show above average performance, while those with negative surprises have below average performance.

Changes in stock price resulting from an earnings surprise can be felt immediately, and the surprise also has a long-term effect. Studies indicate that the effect can persist for as long as a year after the announcement. This means that it does not make sense to buy a stock after the initial price decline of a negative earnings surprise. There is a good chance that the stock will continue to underperform the market for some time. It also indicates that it may not be too late to buy into an attractive company after a better than expected earnings report is released.

Not surprisingly, large firms tend to adjust to surprises more quickly than small firms. Larger firms are tracked by more analysts and portfolio managers, who tend to act quickly.

Firms with a significant quarterly earnings surprise also often have earnings surprises in subsequent quarters. When a firm has a surprise, it often is a sign that other

Firms with Upward Revisions in Earnings Estimates

company (exchange)	I/B/E/S EPS estimate 7/1 ($)	7/29 ($)	change (%)	no. of est.	no. of revs up in mo.	EPS estimate range high ($)	low ($)	price change last qtr (%)	last yr (%)	description
Large Cap (above $1.5 billion)										
Alcan Aluminum Ltd (NY)	0.05	0.08	60	31	5	0.55	(0.35)	17	24	Produces aluminum
U.S. Cellular (NY)	0.08	0.12	50	9	2	0.30	(0.28)	9	(0)	Own, oper cellular phone systems
Int'l Business Machines (NY)	3.03	4.00	32	23	20	4.80	3.45	8	39	Mfrs business machines, computers
Southern Pacific Rail (NY)	0.85	1.00	18	9	5	1.15	0.80	(10)	na	Oper freight railroad network in the West
Tandem Computer (NY)	1.00	1.15	15	15	7	1.33	0.95	17	34	Disk drive, micro-computer sys
General Instrument (NY)	2.61	3.00	15	13	7	3.20	2.50	12	45	Systems, equip to cable, satellite TV ind.
Inland Steel (NY)	1.60	1.82	14	20	8	2.25	1.19	13	48	Integ steel & steel serv
Coca Cola Enterprises (NY)	0.31	0.35	13	13	5	0.42	0.20	(6)	15	Soft drink distributer
Georgia Gulf (NY)	1.70	1.90	12	15	9	2.50	1.50	24	95	Prod commodity chemicals
Apple Computer (NM)	1.45	1.60	10	33	15	1.80	1.11	12	21	Computer systems, tech application
Dana Corp (NY)	2.00	2.20	10	13	9	2.30	1.55	6	4	Manufactures parts for auto industry
Aluminum Co of Amer (NY)	1.37	1.50	9	24	4	2.10	1.00	15	10	Aluminum production; finished alum. prod
Genentech Inc (NY)	1.00	1.09	9	16	6	1.18	0.90	1	16	Devlp health care prods using gene splicing
Lyondell Petroch (NY)	1.13	1.23	9	12	4	1.62	0.45	2	38	Petrochemical, petroleum processor
Eastman Chemical (NY)	2.78	3.00	8	13	4	3.30	2.55	16	na	Chemical co spin-off of Eastman Kodak
Medium Cap ($250 million to $1.5 billion)										
ASARCO Inc (NY)	0.05	0.15	200	13	3	1.30	(1.50)	21	53	Prod silver, copper, lead
Read-Rite Corp (NM)	0.07	0.12	71	5	2	0.15	0.06	10	38	Magnetic recording head for disk drive
Amdahl Corp (AM)	0.30	0.40	33	15	2	0.65	0.00	2	31	Computers, software, communic'n systems
Cobra Golf (NM)	1.48	1.80	22	4	4	1.85	1.52	23	na	Designs, mfrs, mkts golf clubs
Tencor Instruments (NM)	1.10	1.33	21	4	2	1.60	1.00	21	108	Water defect inspection systems
NACCO Industries (NY)	3.55	4.23	19	4	2	4.60	3.50	10	8	Mines/mkts lignite & bituminous coal
Cyrix Corp (NM)	1.50	1.78	19	7	5	1.85	1.50	44	43	IBM-comp micro-process/coprocess

company (exchange)	I/B/E/S EPS estimate			no. of est.	no. of revs up in mo.	EPS estimate range		price change		description
	7/1 ($)	7/29 ($)	change (%)			high ($)	low ($)	last qtr (%)	last yr (%)	
VLSI Technology (NM)	0.89	1.04	17	15	10	1.10	0.88	3	23	Designs, mkts integrated circuits
Novellus Systems (NM)	2.00	2.33	17	12	8	2.35	2.00	1	44	Chemical vapor deposition equip
Quantum Corp (NM)	2.73	3.18	16	12	6	4.00	2.60	(7)	47	Rigid disk drives
Magma Copper (NY)	0.75	0.87	16	16	3	1.45	(0.28)	13	44	Owns/oper copper mines
Modine Mfg (NM)	1.65	1.90	15	8	5	1.95	1.55	5	36	Mfrs, sells heat transfer equip
Oak Industries (NY)	1.48	1.70	15	5	4	1.79	1.50	18	(5)	Mfrs electronic controls & circuits
Robert Half (NY)	1.50	1.70	13	4	3	1.73	1.60	22	84	Personnel placement services
Regal-Beloit Corp (AM)	1.83	2.06	13	4	4	2.10	2.05	2	35	Makes cutting tools, taps, dies, reamers

Small Cap (below $250 million)

company (exchange)	7/1 ($)	7/29 ($)	change (%)	no. of est.	no. of revs up in mo.	high ($)	low ($)	last qtr (%)	last yr (%)	description
Coho Energy (NM)	0.07	0.10	43	4	1	0.18	0.03	22	(28)	Explor, devlp oil & natural gas
Arkansas Best (NM)	0.50	0.60	20	5	2	0.68	0.40	(4)	39	Ship general commodities
Alaska Air Group (NY)	0.85	1.00	18	16	6	1.85	0.47	4	28	U.S. & Alaska airline service
Network Equip (NY)	0.40	0.45	13	7	3	0.65	0.40	14	25	Advanced communicat'ns prods
Tultex Corp (NY)	0.25	0.28	12	9	1	0.40	0.25	(5)	(41)	Mfrs sportswear & yarn
Redman Industries (NM)	2.05	2.28	11	4	2	2.50	2.02	8	na	Producer of manufactured homes
Hauser Chem. Research (NM)	0.20	0.22	10	4	1	0.25	0.03	(12)	(56)	Petrochemical analytical serv
Dura Pharmaceuticals (NM)	0.11	0.12	9	4	2	0.14	0.10	29	121	Specialty pharmaceutical concern
Conmed Corp (NM)	1.02	1.10	8	5	2	1.20	0.75	0	10	Mfg of disposable medical devices
SPX Corp (NY)	1.10	1.18	7	10	4	1.60	1.05	15	5	Automotive components & serv prods
Nuevo Energy (NY)	0.70	0.75	7	9	1	1.25	0.57	6	(16)	Explor, mkt oil & gas
Loyola Capital (NM)	1.53	1.63	7	4	2	1.70	1.55	12	59	Federal stock savings & loan assoc
Sullivan Dental Products (NM)	0.80	0.85	6	5	2	0.93	0.80	10	(23)	Distrib dental prods & equip
Foothill Group A (NY)	1.56	1.64	5	4	4	1.69	1.60	5	17	Financial co specializing in lending
Transmedia Network (NM)	0.43	0.45	5	4	1	0.48	0.36	(11)	78	Restaurant charge cards

na = not available; Exchanges: NY= New York Stock Exchange; AM= American Stock Exchange; NM= Nasdaq National Market; NS= Nasdaq Small Cap

Sources: Stock Investor/Media General; I/B/E/S; and S&P Stock Guide. Data as of July 29, 1994.

similar surprises will follow. This is sometimes referred to as the cockroach effect—like cockroaches, you rarely see just one earnings surprise.

Revisions to earnings estimates lead to price adjustments similar to earnings surprises. When earnings estimates are revised significantly upward—5% or more—stocks tend to show above average performance. Stock prices of firms with downward revisions show below average performance.

Changes in estimates reflect changes in expectations of future performance. Perhaps the economic outlook is better than previously expected, or maybe a new product is selling better than anticipated.

Revisions are often precursors to earnings surprises. As the reporting period approaches, estimates normally converge toward the consensus. A flurry of revisions near the reporting period can indicate that analysts missed the mark and are scrambling to improve their estimates.

The listing on pages 90 and 91 represents the results of a screen for firms with significant earnings estimate revisions. AAII's *Stock Investor*, which contains earnings estimates from I/B/E/S, was used to perform the screening. The screen used data that was current as of July 29, 1994.

About half of the 8,000 securities in *Stock Investor* include earnings estimates. The first screen filtered out those firms with less than four estimates for the current fiscal year. This filter helps to ensure that revisions actually reflect a change in general consensus, not just a change by one or two analysts. However, requiring that a stock have at least four analysts reporting earnings estimates will knock out most of the very small capitalization stocks.

The next filter required that the firm have a change in its current fiscal year estimate over the course of the last month, leaving about 400 firms. The stocks were divided into three market capitalization groups. The percentage change in the estimate from one month to the next was calculated. The 15 firms within each group with the greatest percentage increase in estimate are listed.

The stocks that remained after the screen was applied include a number of cyclical firms experiencing better than expected demand for their products. For example, producers of metals such as Alcan Aluminum, Inland Steel, Aluminum Company of America, and ASARCO at that time were seeing strong enough demand for products that they were able to raise their prices for the first time in years.

Whenever your filter involves the percentage change of a variable, there is a risk that firms with very small base numbers will dominate. With an increase of 200%, ASARCO had the highest percentage revision in the medium-cap group. This jump in percentage change was caused by an increase in earnings estimate from $0.05 to $0.15. When working with percentage changes, it is helpful to use an additional screen to confirm the significance of the change.

The number of estimates for each firm is provided to help gauge the interest in the firm and the meaningfulness of the overall estimates. The larger the firm, the greater the number of analysts that will track it.

The number of revisions upward indicates how many analysts have revised their estimates upward in the last month. When compared to the number of analysts making estimates, this is a confirmation of the significance of the percentage change in estimates. You can put more faith in a revision if a large percentage of the analysts tracking a firm have revised their estimates. VLSI Technology, located in the medium-cap group, had 10 of the 15 analysts tracking the firm revise their estimates upward. This compares with Amdahl, which had only two of its 15 estimates revised upward.

Some investors screen for earnings estimate revisions by looking at the number of revisions. Stock prices of firms with more upward revisions than downward revisions have shown above average returns, while those with more downward revisions tend to underperform.

Examining the range of estimates provides an indication of the consensus within the group of estimates. A wide range of estimates would point to great disagreement among analysts, indicating greater uncertainty and greater chance for an earnings surprise.

The 13 estimates for ASARCO range from a low of –$1.50 to a high of $1.30—a range of $2.80. This is a wide range compared to the Novellus Systems earnings estimates, which range from $2.00 to $2.35. The price move can be more dramatic, however, if an earnings surprise occurs for a firm with a very tight range of earnings estimates.

The last two columns of data help to illustrate the price moves as the market adjusted to changes in expectations. Most of these stocks had experienced fairly strong price moves on both a short-term (three-month) and intermediate-term (one-year) basis. A

Definitions of Screens and Terms

I/B/E/S EPS Estimate: The consensus of analysts' estimates for earning per share as reported by I/B/E/S, a firm that surveys analysts. Reflects the earnings level built into the stock price.

EPS Estimate % Change: The percentage change in the consensus earnings estimate over a one-month period. Prices of firms with positive revisions tend to perform better than average.

No. of Estimates: Number of analysts providing earnings per share estimates. Indicates how widely a firm is followed. Widely followed firms tend to react more quickly to estimate revisions.

No. of Revisions Up in Mo.: The number of analysts who revised their earnings per share estimate for the stock upward during the month. Provides an indication of strength of the earnings revision.

EPS Estimate Range: The highest and lowest earnings per share estimates given by analysts for most recent month-end. Indicates the level of consensus among analysts. The wider the range, the greater the divergence in opinion and the greater the chance for an earnings surprise.

Price Change: The percentage change in the stock price for the last quarter and last year.

larger price change for the last quarter than for the last year would indicate a positive change in price trend. NACCO Industries and Oak Industries are two such examples.

Earnings estimates are important. They embody the expectations built into a stock price. The box below summarizes the main points to keep in mind when dealing with consensus earnings estimates.

Using Consensus Earnings Estimates

Earnings Estimates
Firms with high expected earnings growth tend to underperform the market because it is difficult to meet the market's high expectations. Companies with low earnings expectations tend to do better than expected.

Prices embody current earnings estimates.

Earnings Estimate Revisions
Stock prices of firms with significant upward revisions (5% or more) generally outperform the market. Firms with significant downward revisions underperform the market.

Earnings revisions are often a precursor to earnings surprises. Stock prices react positively to upward revisions.

Earnings Surprise
Stock prices of firms that significantly exceed their earnings expectations (positive earnings surprise) outperform the market, while those with negative earnings surprises underperform.

The earnings surprise effect is long-lasting. The greatest effect of the surprise can be felt immediately, but the effect of the earnings surprise can be seen for as long as a year. The effect of the surprise tends to be longer lasting for negative earnings surprises.

The stock prices of large firms adjust to surprises more quickly than those of small firms.

Earnings surprises often follow in groups—the cockroach effect.

The chance of an earnings surprise is greater if the range of estimates for a company is wide.

The price move can be more dramatic, however, if an earnings surprise occurs for a firm with a very tight range of earnings estimates.

Finding Stocks With Winning Characteristics

One way to develop a strategy is to base it on what has worked in the past. With that in mind, one widely-quoted study examined the characteristics of a group of winning stocks. The goal was to try to find common traits that could be used to develop trading rules for identifying potential winners.

The findings [discussed in an article by Professor Marc Reinganum in the September 1989 *AAII Journal*] are reviewed in Appendix G (on page 101), which discusses the application of the nine trading rules to a database of stocks.

Applying the rules in a series of stock screens, of course, requires a computer. Can the trading rules be adapted to a basic strategy for beginners? This chapter focuses on a basic approach that looks for stocks with some of the major characteristics of stock market winners.

WINNING CHARACTERISTICS

In the original study, nine characteristics of winning stocks were found. However, several characteristics were related, and they can be broken down into four common attributes:

- A price-to-book-value ratio less than 1.0. Book value is total assets less all debt. A price-to-book-value ratio below 1.0 indicates the share price of the firm is below the net assets of the firm—an indication that it may be undervalued.
- Accelerating earnings. An indication that the firm may be starting to turn around.
- High and increasing relative strength. Relative strength is a technical indicator of the price change of the stock relative to the price changes of other stocks. Stocks with strong recent relative strength are considered likely to continue their performance—in other words, they have momentum that is greater than the market's movement.
- Fewer than 20 million common shares outstanding. This characteristic eliminates the very large firms. Stocks with a lesser number of shares outstanding are considered more likely to have stronger price performance once the market "discovers" the stock and starts to bid up share price since there is less liquidity.

An approach based on these characteristics is looking for stocks that are out-of-favor and neglected (low price-to-book-value), are starting to turn around financially (accelerating earnings), are just starting to be recognized by the market (high and rising relative strength), and are likely to register strong price appreciation (lower number of shares outstanding).

THE INITIAL LIST

A big hurdle in applying this approach is developing your initial list. That's because you are looking for stocks that fit several criteria. There are lists of stocks that meet the rules individually, but it would be rare to find a stock that appeared on each list.

Drawing Up an Initial List: Sources of Information

Lists of Stocks With Low Price-to-Book-Values

Standard & Poor's Earnings Guide
Standard & Poor's Corp., 65 Broadway, 8th Floor, New York, N.Y. 10006, 800/221-5277, www.stockinfo.standardpoor.com.
Monthly
Includes summary (one-line) information and focuses on earnings and earnings growth estimates; note that these one-line summaries do not include book value. However, the front includes one short useful list:
Potential Value Plays: These firms are selling at a discount to net tangible book value, a maximum price-earnings ratio (based on next year's earnings estimates) of 15 and a projected 10% increase in earnings.

Value Line Investment Survey
Value Line Publishing Inc., 220 E. 42nd St., New York, N.Y. 10017-5891, 800/634-3583, valueline.com.
Part 1 Summary & Index:
The tables in the back (see index for the page numbers) include this useful list:
Widest Discounts from Book Value: This consists of stocks whose ratios of recent price to book value are the lowest.

Relative Strength Figures

Investor's Business Daily
Investor's Business Daily Inc., P.O. Box 661750, Los Angeles, Calif. 90066-8950; 800/831-2525, www.investors.com.

Daily
Relative strength and other momentum indicators are listed for every stock in the daily stock listings. [Price-earnings ratios, a measure of undervaluation that can be a proxy for low price-to-book-value ratios, are listed for every stock each Wednesday.]

Value Line Investment Survey
Value Line Publishing Inc., 220 E. 42nd St., New York, N.Y. 10017-5891, 800/634-3583, valueline.com.
The one-page descriptions of each stock include a graphical depiction of a stock's relative strength, so you can tell by glancing at the graph whether it is high and rising.

Corporate Financial Data (including book value, quarterly earnings and no. of shares)

Standard & Poor's Stock Reports
Standard & Poor's Corp.
65 Broadway, 8th Floor
New York, N.Y. 10006; 800/221-5277, www.stockinfo.standardpoor.com.
Company reports are found in volumes according to the exchange on which they are traded; presents 10 years of data.

Value Line Investment Survey
Value Line Publishing Inc.
220 E. 42nd St., New York, N.Y. 10017-5891, 800/634-3583, valueline.com.
Analyses over 1,700 common stocks; presents 15 years of data.

The easiest approach is to start with a list of stocks that meet one rule—low price-to-book-value ratios, for instance. Then glance over the full-page reports (in a source such as Value Line Investment Survey) of each of the stocks in the first list, looking to see if any of those stocks fulfill the other requirements.

Lists of firms with low price-to-book-value ratios are suggested as the starting point because book value screens can be harder to find. Only a relatively small number of financially strong firms will be selling for prices that are below book value. Relative strength can also be difficult to find, so restricting your initial search to sources that provide at least one of these two figures will save you some time. However, more firms will have high relative strength (above 70% in the Investor's Business Daily listing) than will pass the book value screen. Information on accelerating earnings and number of shares outstanding are available from sources that provide full-page data listings on individual stocks (such as Value Line and S&P).

Once a potential stock is spotted, the next step is an in-depth evaluation to determine the fair market value. The following example is based on published information that was available in September of 1994, when the approach was applied.

Moog Inc.: An Example

Moog Inc. offers a good example of a firm that meets the restrictions of this approach. The first step was to look at a list of companies that were selling for below book value. Then, each of those stocks was examined using the full-page listings in the Value Line Investment Survey.

Moog passed the first test here, which was to have a high and rising relative strength. The quarterly earnings box was then examined to see if quarterly earnings were trending up. Moog's quarterly earnings were spotty—the firm had rising annual earnings for the prior two years, and in most instances during that time, quarterly earnings relative to the same quarter in the prior year (to account for seasonal adjustments) were rising, but in two instances out of eight they declined.

Lastly, the number of shares outstanding was checked to see if it was below 20 million, and Moog passed this test as well.

Moog is in the aerospace/defense industry and is a manufacturer of components and systems for the defense, commercial transportation (including Boeing and Airbus), and industrial markets. The company suffered, along with the industry, from the cuts in defense spending. Its acquisition of Allied Signal's aerospace actuation business was, according to Value Line, expected to help existing product applications and open up opportunities with aircraft manufacturers; the acquisition is expected to add $0.50 to share earnings in fiscal 1995.

Value Line also noted that its European operations were turning around, due to cost-control measures and a turnaround in the European market. However, these improvements were not expected to add to the bottom line for several quarters. At the time of the screen, the company still faced risk from further declines in the defense budget.

Per Share Data and Financial Ratios

The first item to note is the fiscal year end, which is October 1. The 1994 figures on the valuation worksheet include all of Moog's 1994 fiscal year based on a projection for the last quarter of the fiscal year, made one month into the quarter.

The next item of note is the price trend. In 1992, both its high and low prices were considerably below those of the prior years; more recently, it had come back from that 1992 drop. This is one indication of its price momentum—not surprising given its relative strength trend, which had also risen since 1992.

On a longer-term basis, the price of the stock had dropped considerably from pre-1987 levels, from which it had yet to recover. For instance, in 1987 its high was $19.10 and its low was $8.00. Clearly the stock had been out of favor for quite some time.

Year-by-year earnings per share dropped substantially in 1992. They had started to trend up since then, reaching the 1990 level by mid-1994. That made the five-year earnings growth rate –0.3%; the growth rate since the 1992 low was 43%. Value Line projected 1995 earnings per share of $1.30, most of which was due to its recent acquisition. However, Value Line expected earnings to continue to grow after 1995.

Except in 1992, the firm had paid no dividends. Value Line was not projecting any dividend payments over the next few years. Book value per share remained relatively steady, and the firm's book value at the time of the screen was at its five-year average. In terms of financial ratios, Moog's August 1994 price-earnings ratio at 16.0 was above its five-year average high. Clearly, the market's expectation for the firm was positive, based on a stronger outlook for future earnings. Moog's dividend yield of 0% reflected its lack of dividend payments. The lack of dividend payments also produced a 0% payout ratio.

The 1994 return on equity for Moog of 6.8% was close to the industry average, a sign that the firm might be returning to its pre-1992 levels. Return on equity measures how well the firm is managed both operationally and financially. To boost return on equity, a company must increase its profits from sales, manufacture its goods more efficiently, or increase the level of financial leverage. Moog's use of financial leverage was way above the industry norm. In 1994, its financial leverage increased by 30%, due to the recent acquisition. It is unlikely that this resulted in the most recent increase in return on equity, since the acquisition occurred recently; however, it could be a cause of future increases in return on equity.

Valuing the Company

The bottom of the valuation worksheet provides valuations using the earnings-based model. The dividend-based model is not used here, since no dividends have been paid.

For the earnings-based models, two valuations are provided: one using a 1995 earnings per share projection based on the five-year average growth rate of –0.3% (resulting in a 1995 EPS estimate of $0.85), and one using the Value Line 1995 earnings per share estimate (of $1.30). The five-year averages for the high and low price-earnings ratios were also used in the worksheet.

Valuation Worksheet

Company: MOOG Inc. **Current Price** $ 9.13 **Date (** 8 / 31 / 94 **)**

Ticker MOGA **Exchange** ASE **Current P/E** 16.0 **Current Yield** 0%

Financial Statement & Ratio Analysis

| Per Share Information | Company | | | | | | Industry or Competitor | | Market |
	19 90	19 91	19 92	19 93	19 94	5-year avg	19 94	5-year avg	19 94
Price: High	10.00	9.50	7.60	9.80	9.60	9.30			
Price: Low	5.30	6.00	3.90	5.60	7.00	5.56			
Earnings per Share (EPS)	0.86	0.97	0.41	0.66	0.85	growth rate: −0.3%			
Dividends per Share (DPS)	0.00	0.00	0.28	0.00	0.00	growth rate: 0%			
Book Value per Share (BV)	11.66	12.93	12.62	11.99	12.55	12.35			
Financial Ratios									
Price-Earnings Ratio (P/E): Avg	8.9	8.0	14.0	11.7	9.8	10.5	11.0**	11.4***	
High *(High Price ÷ EPS)*	11.6	9.8	18.5	14.8	11.3	13.2			
Low *(Low Price ÷ EPS)*	6.2	6.2	9.5	8.5	8.2	7.7			
Dividend Yield % (DY): Avg	0.0	0.0	5.4	0.0	0.0	0.0	2.8**	2.8***	
High *(DPS ÷ Low Price)*	0.0	0.0	7.2	0.0	0.0	0.0			
Low *(DPS ÷ High Price)*	0.0	0.0	3.7	0.0	0.0	0.0			
Payout Ratio % (DPS ÷ EPS)	0.0	0.0	68.3	0.0	0.0	0.0	34.0	32.2	
Return on Equity % (EPS ÷ BV)	7.4	7.5	3.2	5.5	6.8	6.1	7.0	8.1	
Financial Leverage* %	122	107	115	107	156	121	33	33	

*long-term debt ÷ equity   **1992   ***1990 through 1992

Earnings-Based Valuation Estimates

Using historical growth rate to project 1995 EPS:

Average high P/E × estimated 19 95 EPS: 13.2 × 0.85 = $11.22 (high valuation estimate)

Average low P/E × estimated 19 95 EPS: 7.7 × 0.85 = $6.54 (low valuation estimate)

Using Value Line 1995 EPS estimate:

Average high P/E × estimated 19 95 EPS: 13.2 × 1.30 = $17.16 (high valuation estimate)

Average low P/E × estimated 19 95 EPS: 7.7 × 1.30 = $10.01 (low valuation estimate)

The valuation using the five-year average growth rate produced a range of $6.54 to $11.22; the valuation using the Value Line 1995 estimate produced a range of $10.01 to $17.16.

Moog's price at that time was $9.13. If Moog at this point were to continue its lackluster five-year average record, it would appear to have been fairly priced based on the valuation model. But if it were turning around, as Value Line suggested, it would have been a bargain. Clearly, a further understanding of the company—its products, competition, and market—would help in forming an opinion about the firm's outlook. The valuation worksheet suggests that the firm merited further investigation.

The basic approach used here adapts the stock winner characteristic rules in the initial screening phase, since it would be difficult to sort through a listing of stocks by hand and come up with those that best fit all the detailed trading rules in the original study. However, it is interesting to note how the firm stacks up according to those rules, and the box below does just that. [Appendix G discusses the rules in more detail.]

CONCLUSION

A careful examination of the assumptions is a critical part of the valuation and will help you identify factors that could be misleading in your final valuation.

While the worksheet examines quantitative factors, it is clear that many subjective factors go into the equation. To judge these factors, it is necessary to go beyond the statistics. Any final decision should be based on a better understanding of the company, its management, and its competitive environment. This can only be accomplished by a thorough reading of the firm's financial reports, as well as the reports and summaries on the firm and its industry.

Stock Market Winners: The Trading Rules and How Moog Stacked Up

Rules*	Did Moog Pass?
1) Price-to-book value less than 1.0	Yes. Current ratio: 0.72
2) Accelerating quarterly earnings—	
Consecutive quarters:	Yes. 19% between March and June; 44% expected between June and September
Quarter-on-quarter:	Yes. 25% between June '94 & '93; 176% expected between September '94 & '93
3) Positive 5-year earnings growth rate	No. Just slightly negative: –0.3%
4) Positive operating margin**	Yes. 12%
5) Relative strength rank of at least 70	Yes. 77%
6) Increase in relative strength rank	Yes. Rank of 52% one quarter prior
7) Stock selling within 15% of two-year high	Yes. 93% of $9.80 two-year high
8) Fewer than 20 million shares outstanding	Yes. 7.7 million shares outstanding

  * *There were 9 trading rules in the study, but one involves proprietary data and is excluded here.*
 ** *Operating margin substituted for pretax profit margin*

Appendix G

Applying the Rules for Stock Market Winners

In September 1989 the *AAII Journal* published an article by Marc Reinganum, titled "Investment Characteristics of Stock Market Winners," which examined the common traits of a group of winning stocks. These types of examinations can be noteworthy if they help to establish financial relationships likely to hold true over time.

The goal was to establish the characteristics common to these stocks prior to their rise to super stock status. Nine trading rules were developed that helped to identify the winners:

- Price-to-book-value ratio less than 1.00;
- Accelerating quarterly earnings;
- Positive five-year growth rate;
- Positive pretax profit margin;
- Relative strength rank of at least 70;
- Relative strength rank of the stock in the current quarter is greater than the rank in the previous quarter;
- O'Neil Datagraph rating of at least 70;
- Stock selling within 15% of its maximum price during the previous two years; and
- Fewer than 20 million common shares outstanding.

The use of these rules or screening criteria produced returns significantly higher than the market. While the group of stocks passing the filter were slightly more risky than the market, the additional risk did not account for the extraordinary returns of the winners.

There can be problems encountered when trying to apply trading rules determined during a specific point in time with a specific group of stocks. This appendix discusses some of the difficulties in trying to interpret and apply these rules to a computer database of stocks in the real market environment.

LOW PRICE-TO-BOOK-VALUE

When examined independently, the first screen requiring that the price-to-book-value ratio be below one produced the highest rate of return. This finding coincides with many studies that show that buying into neglected, out of favor stocks leads to investment success. While the market does a good job of valuing securities in the long run, in the short run it can overreact to information and push the prices away from their true value. Measures such as price-to-book-value ratio, price-earnings ratio, and dividend yield help to identify which stocks may be truly undervalued.

The price-to-book value ratio is determined by dividing market price per share by book value per share. Book value is generally determined by subtracting total liabilities from total assets and then dividing by the number of shares outstanding. It represents the value of the owners' equity based upon the historical accounting activities. If accounting truly captured the current values of the firm, then one would expect the current stock price to sell near this accounting book value. Over the history of a firm, many events occur which can distort the book value figure. For example, inflation may leave the replacement cost of capital goods within the firm way above their stated book value, or the purchase of a firm may lead to the establishment of goodwill, which is an intangible asset boosting the level of book value. Some services are more conservative in reporting book value and may subtract out the value of intangibles such as patents, copyrights, trademarks, or goodwill. Of course it makes these values incomparable with services that include intangibles. Different accounting policies among industries may also come into play when screening for low price-to-book stocks.

AAII's *Stock Investor* program was used to screen for the potential stock market winners, using data that was current as of August 31, 1994. The first screen specified a price-to-book ratio below 1.5, leaving 2,501 companies out of a complete database of 8,145 NYSE, Amex, Nasdaq National Market, and Nasdaq Small Cap stocks. The maximum price-to-book ratio level is higher than the original study so that a slightly larger group of companies would pass the complete set of filters. As a primary screen, specifying a price-to-book ratio below 1.0 led to about 14% of the companies passing the filter, versus about 30% passing the 1.5 price-to-book-value limit.

Valuation levels of stocks vary over time, often dramatically from bear market bottoms to bull market tops. During the depths of a bear market, many firms can be found selling for a price-to-book ratio less than one. In the latter stages of a bull market, few companies other than troubled firms sell for less than book value per share.

EARNINGS MOMENTUM

The low price-to-book screen is very good at identifying neglected firms, but secondary, or conditioning, screens are also needed to help identify which stocks may be poised for a turnaround. Quarterly earnings per share for winners rose on average 46% in the original study and exhibited an increase from the previous quarter's growth rate. Accelerating earnings attract attention, and may be one of the first signs that a company is poised for an upturn.

The earnings measure used in the original study was somewhat crude in that it did not consider the seasonality of quarterly earnings. A more useful technique is to compare one quarter to the same quarter last year, i.e., this year's second quarter is compared to last year's second quarter. Many firms have annual seasonal cycles, either in production or sales. Comparing similar quarters is one way of taking these seasonal changes into consideration.

In our screen, earnings from continuing operations for the most recent two quarters were required to be above their respective quarters last year. This dropped the number of companies down to 824 from the 2,501 passing the low price-to-book-value screen.

To emphasize momentum or acceleration in quarterly earnings, the next criterion specified that the rate of change between the recent quarter and its counterpart last year be greater than the increase between the previous quarter and its counterpart. This momentum screen dropped the number of passing companies down to 383.

The listing on the following pages presents the quarterly earnings per share figures used for the screening. Looking at the raw data can assist in judging the significance of any decisions based upon percentage changes. For example, very small earnings figures can lead to distorted growth rates. Elmer's Restaurant experienced a 400% increase in its latest quarter over the same quarter a year ago, but this increase was based upon a change in earnings per share from one cent to five cents.

MINIMUM FUNDAMENTALS

As further proof that a company's fortunes have turned around, the next two criteria specified a minimum level of company fundamental performance.

The first criterion required that the five-year annual growth rate in earnings per share be positive. Applying this criterion cut the number of firms down to 140. In the original study, the five-year growth rate was based upon the most recent five years of quarterly data. The growth rates used in the screening are based upon the firm's fiscal-year data, which will not show intra-year turnaround as quickly as the trailing quarterly data.

The second criterion required that the pretax profit margin be positive. This is determined by taking sales and subtracting cost of goods sold, operating expenses, interest expenses, and depreciation and amortization, and dividing the result by sales. The gross profit margin was substituted and is calculated by subtracting cost of goods and operating expenses from sales and dividing the result by sales. The gross operating margin is not as stringent as the pretax profit margin used in the original study, but it captures much of the same effect. It represents the type of compromise often necessary when implementing a screening strategy. Requiring a positive gross profit margin brought the number of companies down to 87.

Requiring a positive five-year earnings growth rate or a positive gross operating profit margin by themselves are not very restrictive criteria. However, they help to screen out some of the very weak firms that have some time to go before turning around, if ever. Some investors may be inclined to require not only a positive margin, but a high margin as a criteria. However, it is interesting to note that over the period of the original study, fundamental measures such as profit margins rose substantially during the major price moves. Requiring a high profit margin as a screening criterion would mean missing at least part of this major price advancement.

Stock Market Winners Screen

Company (Exchange)	price-to book-value ratio (×)	quarterly earnings per share				annual EPS grth rate (%)	rel strgth rank (%)	price as % of 52-wk hi (%)	no. of shares out-stand'g (mil)	description
		2nd qtr*		1st qtr*						
		1994 ($)	1993 ($)	1994 ($)	1993 ($)					
Concord Fabrics A (AM)	0.47	0.55	0.36	0.60	0.48	6.5	89	87	2.1	Devlps, designs fabrics
Canandaigua Wine B (NM)	0.53	0.41	0.29	0.35	0.25	54.2	86	98	3.4	Makes dessert, table, & sparkling wines
Dynamics Corp of Am (NY)	0.76	0.45	0.18	0.24	0.16	4.1	83	99	3.9	Mfgs & sells electronic devices
TSR Inc (NM)	0.78	0.10	0.04	0.07	0.00	39.6	87	89	1.5	Operates IBM computer systems
Bindley Western (NM)	0.90	0.34	0.30	0.33	0.30	15.8	86	97	10.8	Wholesales ethical pharmaceuticals
Oglebay Norton (NM)	0.99	2.75	1.12	(0.06)	(0.83)	10.5	90	100	2.5	Lakes shipping: mining & manufacturing
Kings Road Entertain. (NS)	1.05	0.07	0.03	0.03	(0.05)	20.8	81	86	5.3	Devlp, produce, finance motion pictures
FDP Corp (NM)	1.18	0.04	0.01	0.03	(0.03)	35.1	92	94	3.4	Software to market life insurance prods
Schultz Sav-O-Stores (NM)	1.18	0.54	0.45	0.41	0.35	12.6	77	100	2.6	Regional food retailer and wholesaler
FRP Properties (NM)	1.20	0.35	0.17	0.16	0.12	8.4	90	89	4.0	Regulated carrier, real estate
Elmer's Restaurants (NS)	1.21	0.05	0.01	0.02	(0.01)	12.5	93	94	1.8	Owns, operates, sells restaurant franchises
Bell Industries (NY)	1.33	0.57	0.33	0.33	0.22	3.0	83	98	6.3	Distribs, mfrs electronic components
Windmere Corp (NY)	1.35	0.57	0.08	0.03	0.02	5.2	76	94	17.9	Imports & markets personal care prods
Nortek Inc (NY)	1.36	0.44	0.12	0.06	(0.11)	24.6	93	87	12.5	Mfrs commercial & residential bldg prods
Ropak Corp (NM)	1.37	0.53	0.41	(0.06)	(0.11)	39.3	92	93	4.3	Prod plastic shipping containers
Univ Health Serv's B (NY)	1.44	0.57	0.46	0.72	0.60	28.9	92	97	13.1	Owns, operates acute care hospitals

*calendar quarters

Exchanges:
NY = New York Stock Exchange; AM = American Stock Exchange;
NM = Nasdaq National Market; NS = Nasdaq Small Cap

Source: Stock Investor/Media General. All data as of August 31, 1994.

Definitions of Screens and Terms

Price-to-Book-Value Ratio: Market price per share divided by book value (assets less liabilities) per share. A measure of stock valuation relative to net assets. A high ratio might imply an overvalued situation; a low ratio might indicate an overlooked stock.

Quarterly Earnings per Share: Net income from continuing operations of a firm divided by the number of common stock shares outstanding. Comparison of quarterly earnings helps to provide an indication of accelerating earnings.

Annual EPS Growth Rate: Annual growth in earnings per share from continuing operations over the last five fiscal years. A measure of how successful the firm has been in

generating the bottom line, net profit.

Relative Strength Rank: Relative price change, computed here with the most recent quarterly price change given a weight of 40% and the three previous quarters each weighted 20%. The weighted price change is then compared to other stocks over the same time period.

Price as % of 52-Wk High: Most recent market price divided by highest market price over the last 52 weeks.

No. of Shares Outstanding: Total number of shares of stock held by shareholders. Provides an indication of the trading liquidity of the firm.

PRICE MOMENTUM

The next set of criteria help to identify stocks that have already shown upward price movement. Patience is required when selecting stocks using purely contrarian rules. It often takes time for the market to recognize value in the firm. The study indicated that technical measures such as strong and improving relative strength, a current stock price near its high, and a high Datagraphs ranking, point to stocks likely to advance further.

The weighted relative strength ranking was the primary price momentum indicator used in the study. The weighting required that the most recent quarterly price change be given a weight of 40% and the previous three quarters each weighted 20%. The weighted price changes were then ranked for all the stocks and the relative position indicated via percentage rank. Stocks with a 90% relative strength rank had a weighted price change better than 90% of all the firms.

The study indicated that the winners had relative strength rank of 70% or better before their main price move. When this criterion was applied it reduced the number of companies to 33. The study also indicated that it is best if relative strength rank also increased from the previous quarter. While this further screen was not applied to narrow the data set, this is the type of variable that could be investigated after the screening process.

The other price-based screening criterion developed in the study required that the current price be within 15% of the high price for the last two years. This rule reinforces the requirement of price strength. In applying this screen, the 52-week high was used in place of the two-year high. The 52-week high screen is not as strict but the 52-week high is more readily available for most stocks. When applied to our list of stocks it cut the number of firms down to 16.

The original study was performed using the Datagraph books (published by William O'Neil and sold primarily to institutional investors), which include both fundamental and technical data. It was found that the winners usually had a high Datagraph rating in the buy quarter. The Datagraph rating uses a proprietary weighting mix for "reported earnings, capitalization, sponsorship, relative strength, price-volume characteristics, group rank and other factors." Since most individuals will not have access to this charting and data service, it was not used in the screen. It is worth noting, however, that the other rules seem to reflect much of the information contained within the Datagraph rating.

Limited Float

This criterion examines the number of shares outstanding, often termed the float. The study found that 90% of the firms had fewer than 20 million shares outstanding before their main price rise. The midpoint or median figure was 5.7 million shares, which doubled during the two years that each "winning" stock was held. This probably indicates many of the firms split their shares during their big price increase.

Some investors look for a stock to have a limited float with the belief that the price move on positive information will be magnified by a limited number of shares available. Applying this screening criterion did not cause any firms to drop out. It seems that in today's market the other screening criteria did a good job of filtering out the larger firms that have more shares outstanding.

The list of stocks passing all the screens is presented in the listing. They are ranked on the price-to-book-value ratio. The list represents a diverse set of relatively small firms. Like all screens, this list provides a beginning point for further in-depth analysis.

Conclusion

Examining the characteristics of past stock market winners might prove interesting. But using all of the rules may lead to a very restrictive screen in the present. Screens can also be in some ways contradictory. In this case, there is a strong price-to-book neglect screen tied to look-at-me earnings and stock price movements.

But it is hard to argue with screens that try to find neglected stocks on the verge of a fundamental and technical turnaround.

Adapting the Lynch Principles to the Basic Approach

One of the best ways to learn about investing is to follow an example—preferably someone with a successful track record. One popular investment guru, Peter Lynch, former portfolio manager of the Fidelity Magellan Fund, has written two books that discuss the primary investment principles he followed when managing the enormously popular fund. This chapter focuses on a basic approach that follows his rules of thumb for beating the pros. Appendix H (on page 115) outlines the principles in more detail and discusses their use when screening a database of stocks.

THE LYNCH PRINCIPLES

The Stock-Picking Checklist (see page 121) of Appendix H summarizes the main principles outlined by Mr. Lynch in his two books, "One Up on Wall Street" and "Beating the Street."

Mr. Lynch advocates a "bottom-up approach," which means that you start your search process at the ground floor, looking for individual companies that appear to have promising products or services. Once you have identified a promising candidate, you then carefully research and analyze it, checking first to see if your initial impression is supported by financial evidence and the firm's competitive environment and if the stock can be purchased at a reasonable price.

This process entails searching for candidates one by one, rather than beginning with a list of candidates that may have passed an initial screen. How do you find initial candidates? Mr. Lynch strongly advises that you put your own experience and knowledge to work, looking at companies with products and services with which you are familiar and thus more capable of analyzing.

Once you have found a promising candidate, he suggests that, among other things, you look for the following features:

- A price-earnings ratio relative to the earnings growth rate of less than 0.5
- A price-earnings ratio that is in the lower range of its historical average and below the industry average
- Stable and consistent earnings
- Low levels of debt

Sources of Information

Pre-Screened List of Firms With Low P/Es Relative to Earnings Growth Rate

Standard & Poor's Earnings Guide

(Monthly) Includes summary (1-line) information and focuses on earnings, earnings growth estimates. The front periodically includes:
Strong EPS & Dividends to P/E Ratio: These are firms whose 5-year annual earnings growth rate plus the current dividend yield relative to their price-earning ratio is greater than 2. [Seeking firms with a ratio above 2 is equivalent to the Peter Lynch rule that uses the inverse formula—dividing the price-earnings ratio by the earnings growth rate—and seeks ratios below 0.5.] These firms also must pay dividends and five years of positive earnings.

Lynch's Laws: Finding Information

Price Earnings Ratios, Earnings Growth, and Historical Earnings: The three most complete sources for historical corporate financial information are Moody's Handbook of Common Stock, Standard & Poor's Stock Reports, and the Value Line Investment Survey. In addition, don't forget the primary source—the company's own annual financial reports. Corporate annual reports will include both summary and detailed financial statements; the summaries cover a five- or 10-year span. More detailed financial statements are available in the 10K. Both reports can be requested from the company.
Comparing Co. P/Es to Industry P/Es: S&P's Industry Reports provides a monthly review of 80 industries. In addition, data on industry indexes is provided in The Wall Street Journal (Dow Jones Industry Groups daily), Investor's Business Daily (Industry Prices every Tuesday), and Barron's (a listing of the Dow Jones Industry Groups is given in the Market Statistics Section). Value Line reports industry ratios in its industry analysis sections but these can be dated.

Balance Sheet Strength: The sources listed for price-earnings ratios and historical earnings are good sources for balance sheet strength.
Cash Position: The sources listed for price-earnings ratios and historical earnings are good sources for cash position. The monthly S&P Stock Guide reports current cash holdings, as well as long-term debt (Peter Lynch subtracts long-term debt per share from cash per share to determine a firm's net cash per share position.)
Level of Institutional Holdings: Value Line's full-page company summaries include a box called "Institutional Decisions" that reports the number of shares held by institutions. S&P's Stock Guide gives both the number of shares held by institutions and the number of institutions holding shares in the company. S&P Stock Reports and Moody's Handbook also report the percentage held by institutions.
Insider-Buying: Value Line's full-page company summaries include a box called "Insider Decisions" that reports insider buying.
Company Share Buybacks: Value Line often discusses buybacks in the write-up section. Also check in Value Line to see if shares outstanding has been decreasing over time, indicating company buybacks. Similar information is available in S&P Stock Reports and Moody's Handbook.

Addresses for Sources

Value Line Investment Survey, Value Line Publishing Inc., 220 E. 42nd St., New York, N.Y. 10017-5891; 800/634-3583, valueline.com

Standard & Poor's Stock Reports, Standard & Poor's Earnings Guide, Standard & Poor's Industry Reports, 65 Broadway, 8th Floor,New York, N.Y. 10006; 800/221-5277, www.stockinfo.standardpoor.com

Moody's Handbook of Common Stock, 99 Church St., New York, N.Y. 10007; 800/342-5647, www.moodys.com

Other positive signs include: high net cash per share relative to the stock price; low levels of institutional holdings; insider buying by a number of insiders; and company share buybacks. Mr. Lynch also favors smaller firms over larger firms and dislikes "hot" stocks in "hot" industries.

Once you have spotted a promising candidate, the information source list can help you gather the information you need for further analysis. Many of these sources may be available in your local library. However, don't forget one of the single best sources of information—the company itself, from which you can request its financial reports. Notice that there is one pre-screened list that appears in the S&P Earnings Guide (firms that meet Mr. Lynch's low price-earnings ratio to growth rate rule-of-thumb)—you may find a firm or two listed there in which you are familiar with its product or service.

Once you have spotted a potential stock, the next step is an in-depth evaluation.

INTEL CORP.: AN EXAMPLE

Intel Corp. offers an example of how a firm could be analyzed using the Lynch principles as a guide. Intel was selected because it appeared on the S&P Earnings Guide pre-screened list at the time of the analysis, in October of 1994, and because it is in the computer sector—a sector quite familiar to at least half of the authors (John Bajkowski is editor of AAII's *Computerized Investing*).

A summary of Intel in late 1994:

Intel is best known as the designer and manufacturer of the micro-processor or "brain" that drives most of the IBM-based personal computers. Intel's processors, controllers, and memory chips are also heavily used in communications, automation, and other electrical equipment.

Intel is, of course, a technology stock, a "hot" industry. Typically, the product life cycle within the industry is very short and getting shorter. Intel spent 11% of its $11 billion in sales on research and development to advance its products and keep one step ahead of its competitors. Intel at that time was facing competition from competitors cloning its main processors, and from a new generation of processor chips from companies such as IBM and Motorola. The chip business is very cut-throat, and Intel has used the court system, faster product introductions and lower prices to meet the competition.

At the time of the analysis, Intel's future growth in earnings was dependent on greater volume of sales with lower profit margins, common to industries that reach a more mature phase. Intel at that time was pushing adoption of its latest generation chip, Pentium, at a much faster rate than earlier designs and rolling out more efficient plants to help keep costs down.

PER SHARE INFO & FINANCIAL RATIOS

Value Line was used as the primary source for financial information. Figures for 1994 were based on Value Line projections for the remainder of the year.

The first item of note is the price trend. Intel's stock price rose steeply and steadily from 1991 through 1993; in late 1994, it had fallen from its 1994 high earlier in the year of $73.50.

Year-by-year earnings per share steadily increased since 1990, with an average five-year growth rate of 38.6%. That certainly meets the Lynch rule of thumb of stable and consistent earnings; on the other hand, this high growth rate could put it in the "hot stock" category. More recently, however, earnings growth slowed: between 1993 and 1994, earnings went from $5.16 to $5.90 per share—an increase of 14%. Value Line predicted a continuation of that 14% growth rate, with a 1995 earnings per share projection of $6.75. Interestingly, this slowdown made Intel more appealing from the Lynch perspective—Intel might no longer be the "hot" stock of several years ago.

Intel did not start paying dividends until 1992, when it paid a $0.05 dividend in the last quarter. Dividends were paid for the full year in both 1993 and 1994, during which dividends were increased from $0.20 to $0.22—a 10% increase. While that time span is too short to indicate any long-term trend, it did appear that Intel was now committed to paying some level of dividends. Value Line estimates dividends per share of $0.27 in 1995. The fact that this firm started to pay dividends—and they were increasing—may have been another sign that this firm was moving away from its quick-growth phase and was starting to mature.

In terms of financial ratios, Intel's price-earnings ratio, at 11.1, was below its five-year average high. Clearly, the market's expectation for the firm had dropped, based on its declining earnings growth rate. How did Intel's price-earnings ratio compare with the industry average? Value Line's price-earnings ratio for the industry was dated—1993 is the most recently reported figure. Intel's price-earnings ratio was lower, however, than the 1994 industry average of 16.8 reported by S&P Industry Reports. With Intel's price-earnings ratio below its historical average and the industry average, it may have been an indication of undervaluation.

Intel's October 1994 dividend yield of 0.4% was so low that it is probably insignificant—no investor was buying this stock for the dividend.

The low level of dividends resulted in a very low payout ratio of 3.7% in 1994—below the industry average of 17.0%.

The 1994 return on equity of 25.1% for Intel was much higher than the industry average, and had increased over time, although it had slid back from its 1993 high of 28.8%.

Return on equity measures how well the firm is managed both operationally and financially. To boost return on equity, a company must increase its profits from sales, manufacture its goods more efficiently, or increase the level of financial leverage. Intel's use of financial leverage (long-term debt divided by equity) was far below the industry norm—its five-year average was 6.4% compared to an industry average of 17.2%. Intel therefore appeared to be maintaining its high return on equity from increasing sales—reflected in the year-by-year earnings increases.

What about some of the other Lynch Laws that are not found on the valuation worksheet? Using Value Line as a source, Intel violated most:

Valuation Worksheet*

Company: Intel Corp.   **Current Price $** 61.50   **Date (** 9/30/94 **)**

Ticker INTC   **Exchange** NMS   **Current P/E** 11.1   **Current Yield** 0.4%

Financial Statement & Ratio Analysis

Per Share Information	Company					5-year avg	Industry or Competitor		Market
	19 90	19 91	19 92	19 93	19 94		19 94	5-year avg	current
Price: High	26.00	29.60	45.80	74.30	73.50				
Price: Low	14.00	18.90	23.30	42.80	56.00				
Earnings per Share (EPS)	1.6	1.91	2.51	5.16	5.9	growth rate: 38.6%			
Dividends per Share (DPS)	0.00	0.00	0.05*	0.20	0.22	growth rate: 10.0%**			
Book Value per Share (BV)	8.99	10.83	13.01	17.94	23.55	14.86			
Financial Ratios									
Price-Earnings Ratio (P/E): Avg	12.5	12.7	13.8	11.3	11.0	12.3	14.4***	18.75†	18.0
High (High Price ÷ EPS)	16.3	15.5	18.2	14.4	12.5	15.4			
Low (Low Price ÷ EPS)	8.8	9.9	9.3	8.3	9.5	9.1			
Dividend Yield % (DY): Avg	0.0	0.0	0.0	0.4	0.3	0.4**	0.4***	0.5†	2.9
High (DPS ÷ Low Price)	0.0	0.0	0.0	0.5	0.4	0.4**			
Low (DPS ÷ High Price)	0.0	0.0	0.0	0.3	0.3	0.3**			
Payout Ratio % (DPS ÷ EPS)	0.0	0.0	0.0	3.9	3.7	3.8**	17.0	13.0	
Return on Equity % (EPS ÷ BV)	17.8	17.6	19.3	28.8	25.1	21.7	10.0	12.5	
Financial Leverage %	9.6	8.2	4.6	5.7	3.8	6.4	15.1	17.2	

*one quarter only   **2-year figures   ***1993   †1990-1993

Valuation Estimates

Model based on earnings (using Value Line 1995 EPS estimate):

Average high P/E × estimated 19 95 EPS: ___15.4___ × ___6.75___ = ___$103.95___ (high valuation estimate)

Average low P/E × estimated 19 95 EPS: ___9.1___ × ___6.75___ = ___$61.42___ (low valuation estimate)

Model based on dividends (using 1995 DPS estimate based on dividend growth rate):

Estimated 19 95 annual DPS ÷ average low DY: ___0.24___ ÷ ___0.003___ = ___$80.00___ (high valuation estimate)

Estimated 19 ___ annual DPS ÷ average high DY: ___0.24___ ÷ ___0.004___ = ___$60.00___ (low valuation estimate)

Use decimal form for DY. For instance 5.4% would be 0.054.

*The figures in this worksheet do not reflect the 2-for-1 stock split in 1995.

- Intel was not small—it had a market capitalization (419 million common shares outstanding times $61.50 share price) of over $25 billion;
- It had a low level of net cash per share relative to its stock price—its net cash per share position was $4.59 (cash assets of $2,300 million less $375 million in long-term debt, divided by 419 million common shares outstanding) compared to its $61.50 per share stock price;
- Over 71% of its shares were held by institutions (298 million shares held by institutions divided by 419 million common shares outstanding);
- There had been no insider buying decisions over the past year;
- No share buybacks were mentioned in the Value Line company summary, and over time, the number of shares outstanding has increased; and
- It was (and is) in a hot and highly competitive industry.

Valuing the Company

The bottom of the valuation worksheet provides valuations using both the earnings-based model and the dividends-based model.

For the earnings-based models, the Value Line estimate for 1995 earnings were used on the worksheet, since this is a more conservative estimate. A projection based on Intel's five-year growth rate of 38.6% would suggest 1995 earnings of $8.17; however, given the slowdown in earnings growth, this higher earnings projection is probably too optimistic.

Using the Value Line projections, the model produces a high valuation of $103.95 and a low valuation estimate of $61.42.

The dividend-based model uses a 1995 dividends per share projection of $0.24 based on the 10% increase over the past year. Although this time period does not indicate a trend, it does produce a more conservative estimate than the Value Line 1995 projection of $0.27. The dividend-based model produces a valuation range of $60.00 to $80.00. However, given the insignificant dividend yield paid by Intel, this model is less useful in valuing this stock—investors were not making decisions based on the dividend-paying capability of this firm, and therefore dividends were unlikely to play a significant role in the pricing of the stock.

Intel's price at that time of $61.50 was close to the low valuation indicated by the earnings-based model and suggested that the firm may have been undervalued. Intel also met some of the Lynch rules-of-thumb, but not all, as outlined above. These preliminary analyses suggested that the stock may merit further investigation but with some skepticism; certainly familiarity with the industry would be helpful.

Conclusion

A careful examination of the assumptions is a critical part of the valuation and will help you identify factors that could be misleading in your final valuation. While the worksheet examines quantitative factors, it is clear that many subjective factors go into the equation. To judge these factors, it is necessary to go beyond the statistics. Any final decision should be based on a better understanding of the company, its management, and its competitive environment. This can only be accomplished by a thorough reading of the firm's financial reports, as well as the reports and summaries on the firm and its industry.

Appendix H

Stock Screening à la Peter Lynch

Examining the investment techniques of successful money managers can prove insightful when trying to establish or refine your personal techniques. In this chapter, we explore the techniques of investment manager Peter Lynch and how they can be applied to screen a computerized database of stocks.

LYNCH'S LAWS

In his two books, "One Up on Wall Street" and "Beating the Street," Peter Lynch describes the analytical process that led to his success at the helm of Fidelity's Magellan fund:

- *Stick with industries and companies you know and understand.* Getting ideas is a critical starting point for a bottom-up stockpicker like Peter Lynch. He advocates looking around at companies and products for stock ideas and then performing in-depth analysis to determine if the stock is a buy. This would be contrasted with a top-down approach that starts the analysis with an overall economic forecast that leads to sectors, industries, and finally companies expected to perform well.

  In looking for ideas, Lynch favors areas that you understand and where your intimate knowledge is a competitive advantage. For example, if you are a pharmacist, use your knowledge to analyze the drug industry. Also notice trends around you—is a new store in the mall a hit? If so, investigate it. Leverage your knowledge as a consumer, hobbyist, and professional in your investments.

- *Do your research before investing.* Lynch observes that many people follow a hunch or a tip and invest in a company without doing any research. Very often these are the same individuals who spend many hours researching which coffee maker is the best on the market and scouring the papers to discover which store offers the best price.

- *Is it a buy?* Finding a good company is only half of the battle in making a successful investment. Buying at a reasonable price is the other. Lynch looks at both earnings and assets when it comes to valuing stocks. An earnings examination focuses on the ability of the company to earn future income. The greater the earnings prospects, the more valuable the company. Increasing earnings will translate to increasing prices. Assets are important in determining the base value of a company should it be split up and sold off in pieces.

- *Carefully consider the price-earnings ratio.* The earnings potential of a company is a primary determinant of company value. At times, the market may get ahead of itself and overprice even a stock with great prospects. The price-earnings ratio helps to keep your perspective in check. The ratio compares the current price to the most recently reported earnings. Stocks with good prospects should sell with higher price-earnings ratios than stocks with poor prospects.

- *How does the price-earnings ratio compare to its historical average?* By studying the pattern of price-earnings ratios over a period of several years, you can develop a sense of the normal level for the company. This knowledge should help you avoid buying into a stock if the price gets ahead of the earnings or send an early warning that it may be time to take some profits in a stock you own. If a company does everything well, you may not make any money on the stock if you paid too much for it.
- *How does the price-earnings ratio compare to the industry average?* Comparing a company's price-earnings ratio to that of the industry may help reveal if the company is a bargain. At a minimum, it leads to questions as to why the company is priced differently. Is it a poor performer in the industry, or is it just neglected? Lynch's ideal investment is a neglected niche company, controlling a market segment, in an unglamorous industry that would be difficult and time-consuming for a competitor to break into.
- *How does the price-earnings ratio compare to its earnings growth rate?* Companies with better prospects should sell with higher price-earnings ratios. A useful valuation technique is to compare the price-earnings ratio to the earnings growth rate. A price-earnings ratio of half the level of historical earnings growth is considered attractive, while ratios above two are considered unattractive.

  Lynch refines this measure by adding the dividend yield to the earnings growth. This adjustment acknowledges the contribution that dividends make to an investor's return. The ratio is calculated by dividing the price-earnings ratio by the sum of the earnings growth rate and the dividend yield. With this modified technique, ratios above one are considered poor, while ratios below 0.5 are considered attractive.
- *How stable and consistent are the earnings?* It is important to examine the historical record of earnings. Stock prices cannot deviate very long from the level of earnings, so the pattern of earnings growth will help to reveal the stability and strength of the company. Ideally, earnings should move up consistently.
- *Avoid hot companies in hot industries.* Lynch prefers to invest in companies with earnings expanding at moderately fast rates (20% to 25%) in non-growth industries. Extremely high levels of earnings growth rates are not sustainable but continued high growth may be factored into the price. A high level of growth for a company and industry will attract a great deal of attention from both investors, who bid up the stock price, and competitors, who provide a more difficult business environment.
- *What is the level of institutional holdings?* Lynch feels that the bargains are located

among the stocks neglected by Wall Street. The lower the percentage of shares held by institutions and the lower the number of analysts following the stock, the better.

- *How large is the firm?* Small firms have more upside potential than large firms. Small firms can easily expand in size while large firms are limited. A small firm like Starbucks can double in size much more easily than a large firm such as General Electric.
- *How strong is the balance sheet?* A strong balance sheet provides maneuvering room as the company expands or experiences trouble. Lynch is especially wary of bank debt, which can usually be called in by the bank on demand.
- *What is the level of net cash per share?* Lynch likes to look at the net cash per share to help discover both a support for the stock price and the financial strength of the company. The net cash per share is calculated by adding the level of cash and cash equivalents, subtracting the long-term debt, and dividing the result by the number of shares outstanding.
- *Are insiders buying the stock?* Insider buying of shares is a positive sign, especially if it is spread among a number of individuals. While insiders may have many reasons for selling holdings, they generally buy stock when they feel it is an attractive investment.
- *Is the company buying back shares?* Lynch favors companies that buy back their shares over companies that choose to expand into unrelated businesses. Share buybacks become an issue once companies start to mature and have cash flow that exceeds their capital needs. The share buyback will help to support the stock price and is usually performed when management feels that the current stock price is favorable.

APPLYING THE LYNCH SCREEN

While Peter Lynch is a bottom-up, kick-the-tires type of stockpicker, some of his principles are useful screening criteria. Our first screen excluded financial firms. Peter Lynch is a big fan of financial stocks and presents a series of screens he uses to help select banks and savings and loans in "Beating the Street." We had to exclude them from the general screen, however, because their financial statements cannot be directly compared to other firms. AAII's *Stock Investor* program was used to perform the screen using data that was current as of September 30, 1994; we were left with 5,751 non-financial companies out of a total of 8,123 stocks.

Price-earnings ratios are an important aspect to Lynch's analysis and make an excellent primary screen. Our screen used the ratio of price-earnings to the earnings growth rate plus the dividend yield. A ratio less than or equal to 0.50 was specified as a cut-off, leaving 441 companies.

Lynch is wary of companies growing too quickly, so the next filter specified a maximum earnings per share growth rate of 50%. The number of firms passing this filter was 258.

The final filter required that the long-term debt-to-capital ratio for each company be

Low P/E to Earnings Growth Stocks

company (exchange)	modified P/E to EPS growth (×)	P/E ratio (×)	EPS growth rate (%)	div yield (%)	long-term debt to cap (%)	shares held by inst'ns (%)	net cash per share ($)	price ($)	price as % of 52-wk high (%)	description
Large Cap (above $1.5 billion)										
Intel Corp (NM)	0.22	11.1	49.5	0.4	5.4	73.7	4.88	61.50	83	Semicond components, systems
General Dynamics (NY)	0.25	11.2	41.3	3.2	14.6	55.9	12.63	43.75	88	Military marine & aircraft
Sun Co (NY)	0.37	13.7	30.3	6.3	26.8	53.6	(5.73)	28.75	82	Energy resources integrated petro coal
NFC Plc ADR (AM)	0.43	14.8	31.1	3.6	36.6	0.2	(0.24)	15.38	72	Transport, logistics, home delivery serv
Magna Int'l A (NY)	0.47	12.3	23.9	2.0	10.1	75.3	0.20	36.88	68	Automotive components, systems
Medium Cap ($250 million to $1.5 billion)										
IP Timberlands (NY)	0.14	4.1	18.1	11.6	0.2	1.2	0.20	24.88	80	Forest resource management
Bowne & Co (AM)	0.16	7.8	45.3	2.0	4.3	53.3	0.53	18.00	63	Finance & corporation printing
Family Dollar Stores (NY)	0.28	9.6	31.0	3.0	0.0	64.7	0.11	11.38	62	Operates discount stores
Scitex Corp (NM)	0.28	14.0	48.0	2.3	0.1	29.7	6.39	22.50	84	Computer imaging systems
Briggs & Stratton (NY)	0.30	9.9	30.4	2.6	15.7	71.6	10.09	70.25	78	Mfrs air cooled engines & auto locks
Standard Microsys'ms (NM)	0.30	11.8	38.8	0.0	6.0	40.6	1.96	19.88	74	Mfrs semiconductor circuits
Lattice Semicon (NM)	0.32	15.3	47.2	0.0	0.0	68.2	5.65	18.50	75	Programmable logic devices
Clarcor Inc (NY)	0.33	15.2	42.7	3.1	19.0	52.2	(1.18)	20.25	90	Mobile & environ'l filtration prods
Instrument Systems (NY)	0.35	10.6	30.4	0.0	12.6	45.7	0.77	7.88	81	Mfrs diversified instruments
Rayonier Timberlands (NY)	0.35	6.5	4.3	14.3	32.8	0.2	0.00	35.25	88	Marketing, sale of timber
Ballard Medical Prods (NY)	0.37	15.3	41.4	0.5	0.0	38.1	0.94	10.38	56	Disposable medical products
XTRA Corp (NY)	0.37	17.8	46.4	1.1	51.1	63.1	na	51.25	96	Tractor-trailer, cargo contain leasing
Lancaster Colony (NM)	0.43	17.8	40.2	1.4	12.2	73.1	(0.07)	35.00	89	Mfrs food and auto products
Church & Dwight (NY)	0.47	18.0	36.5	1.9	4.3	47.0	(0.04)	23.00	79	Mfrs, mkts soap & cleaning prods
Weatherford Int'l (AM)	0.47	20.0	42.8	0.0	6.3	65.0	(0.83)	12.38	84	Equip for petroleum industry
Champion Enterprises (AM)	0.48	14.1	29.1	0.0	5.7	36.7	1.07	39.25	99	Hold'g co, Champion Home Builders

company (exchange)	modified P/E to EPS growth (×)	P/E ratio (×)	EPS growth rate (%)	div yield (%)	long-term debt to cap (%)	shares held by inst'ns (%)	net cash per share ($)	price ($)	price as % of 52-wk high (%)	description
Shadow Stocks (small firms with lower institutional interest)										
Norex America (AM)	0.08	1.8	21.7	0.0	14.6	1.4	(6.41)	9.25	82	Mkts, provides leisure cruises
Huffman Koos (NM)	0.17	6.4	37.2	0.0	18.7	12.8	na	7.75	86	Specialty furniture retailer
SBE Inc (NM)	0.22	9.1	40.8	0.0	0.0	15.9	na	7.50	60	Designs, sells computer hardware
Diodes Inc (AM)	0.26	11.7	45.1	0.0	3.6	5.4	0.22	5.50	55	Semiconductor devices
CCA Industries (NM)	0.27	11.0	41.4	0.0	7.1	11.2	0.84	4.38	48	Makes specialty cosmetic products
Shelter Components (AM)	0.28	9.2	32.2	0.4	28.4	58.4	(2.14)	12.00	73	Mfrs, sells, distrib prods for houses
Genovese Drug (AM)	0.35	11.6	30.9	2.2	0.0	14.2	(3.44)	11.00	79	Drug store chain in NYC
Prima Energy (NM)	0.35	11.8	33.8	0.0	6.0	8.3	na	13.75	81	Explor, devlp, prod oil & gas
Comcoa Inc (NM)	0.37	12.0	32.8	0.0	0.0	6.4	0.28	14.00	89	Rent-A-Center
Craftmade Int'l Inc (NM)	0.42	15.1	36.1	0.2	0.0	22.7	0.03	10.44	84	Designs, distrib, mkts ceiling fans
Jennifer Convertible (NM)	0.42	13.6	32.5	0.0	0.4	7.2	2.19	7.75	48	Sells sofabeds
Methode Electr'cs B (NM)	0.48	20.0	41.0	0.5	0.0	11.6	1.13	20.00	100	Mfrs electronic component devices
Refac Techn'gy Dev. (AM)	0.48	9.9	20.5	0.0	0.0	17.6	2.75	7.13	60	Administers int'l technology licenses
Xscribe Corp (NM)	0.48	10.7	22.1	0.0	7.2	8.0	na	2.56	44	Hard-, software for computer-aided sys
Western Beef (NM)	0.49	10.6	21.6	0.0	17.4	9.4	(0.80)	7.50	52	Wholesale meat and poultry
Jones Medical Indus (NM)	0.50	11.6	22.1	1.3	1.6	27.6	(0.08)	7.75	44	Prod branded & generic ethical drugs
Prime Medical Corp (NM)	0.50	12.0	24.1	0.0	7.4	6.9	na	3.13	86	Estab & mgmt of cardiac rehab centers

na = not available
Exchanges:
NY = New York Stock Exchange
AM = American Stock Exchange
NM = Nasdaq National Market
NS = Nasdaq Small Cap

Sources: Stock Investor/Media General; S&P Stock Guide. All data as of September 30, 1994.

Definitions of Screens and Terms

Modified P/E to EPS Growth: Current price-earnings ratio divided by the sum of the historical earnings growth rate and dividend yield. Ratios below 0.5 are considered attractive. Ratios above 1 are considered poor.

P/E Ratio: Market price per share divided by most recent 12 months' earnings per share. A measure of the market's expectations regarding the firm's earnings growth and risk.

EPS Growth Rate: Annual growth in earnings per share from total operations over the last five fiscal years. A measure of how successful the firm has been in generating the bottom line, net profit.

Dividend Yield: Indicated annual dividend divided by market price.

Long-Term Debt to Capital: Long-term debt divided by the total of long-term debt and preferred and common equity. Provides a measure of the financial strength of the company. The lower the figure, the stronger the balance sheet.

Shares Held by Institutions: Percentage of shares outstanding that are held by institutions. Provides an indication of the level of Wall Street interest in the stock.

Net Cash per Share: The total of all cash and cash equivalents less long-term debt, divided by the number of shares outstanding. Provides an indication of the financial strength of the company and a support for the stock price.

Price: Most recent market price as of September 30, 1994.

Price as % of 52-Wk. High: Most recent market price divided by highest market price over the last 52 weeks.

less than its industry average, leaving 125 firms.

The screens we applied seemed to favor smaller firms. Of the 125 firms that passed the screen, only five were large-cap stocks—16 were medium-cap, and 104 were small-cap. All of the large- and medium-cap firms that passed the filter are shown, ranked in ascending order by the modified price-earnings to growth ratio. Within the small cap area, 17 of the stocks passing the screens were Shadow Stocks, AAII's term for non-financial stocks that are small, have low institutional interest, and have had positive annual earnings for the two previous years.

Most of the companies passing the screens had relatively low price-earnings ratios when compared to the current market level of 18.0. The historical growth rates, however, were well above average, with many ranging between 30% and 40% per year. These are historical growth rates and are not sustainable for a long period of time; some are due to special situations. General Dynamic's growth rate of 41.3% was due to a one-time earnings boost in 1993. Looking only at earnings from continuing operations and the year-by-year earnings figures would present a better picture of earnings growth and consistency.

The dividend yield for two of the securities—IP Timberlands and Rayonier Timberlands—should clue an investor in to a special situation. Both of the securities are limited partnerships created to manage the lumber resources of International Paper and

Stock-Picking Checklist

• Invest only in industries and companies you understand and know the specific reason that you are buying the stock.	➤ Your analysis should center on the factors that will move the stock price
• How does the price-earnings ratio compare to the growth rate in earnings and dividends?	➤ Look for low P/Es compared to earnings growth plus the dividend yield
• How does the price-earnings ratio compare to its historical average?	➤ Look for P/E in lower range of historical average
• How does the price-earnings ratio compare to the industry?	➤ Look for P/E below industry average
• How stable and consistent are the earnings?	➤ Study the pattern of earnings, especially how they reacted during a recession
• How strong is the balance sheet?	➤ Look for a low level of debt, especially bank debt
• What is the cash position?	➤ Net cash per share should be high relative to stock price
• Avoid hot companies in hot industries.	➤ Be wary of earnings growth rates above 50%
• Big companies have small moves, small companies have big moves.	➤ Small companies should be favored in your search, they have more upside potential
• What is the level of institutional holdings?	➤ Look for low percentage of shares held by institutions and number of analysts following stocks
• Are insiders buying stock?	➤ Insider buying by a number of insiders is a positive sign
• Is the company buying back shares?	➤ If so, this will support the stock price and probably indicates the company has been ignored, but management is confident

Rayonier, respectively. These are partnerships structured with finite lives and they highlight the importance of in-depth analysis after any basic screen.

The ratio of long-term debt to capital is generally lower for small-cap stock than for the medium- and large-cap stocks. Small-cap stocks have a more difficult time raising capital through the bond market than larger stocks and often turn to banks for capital. A close examination of the financial statements, especially in the notes to the financial statement, should help to reveal the use of bank debt.

A large number of the listed companies have very high percentage of shares held by institutions, a negative in Lynch's opinion.

Net cash per share highlights a potential hidden asset for a number of companies and is of greater interest for companies that are distressed, turnaround potentials, or asset plays.

Only a basic level of screening was performed when presenting the Lynch-based screens. Much of the analysis advocated by Peter Lynch is subjective in nature, requiring hands-on analysis. As Peter Lynch stresses, it is possible to succeed at investing, but you must be willing to do your work.